To David and Susan

Foreword

I first met Louis Sternburg some thirty years ago in my role as Assistant Resident in Medicine at Massachusetts General Hospital, where I was serving on the polio service. He is without a doubt the most unusual patient that I have ever known. At our initial encounter, we were both early in our careers and family responsibilities. Indeed, one of the difficulties that I had as the personal physician not only to Lou but to many others during that polio epidemic of 1955 was my realization that many of these patients, so similar to me in age, goals, and career paths, would be profoundly disabled and perhaps even die. At the same time, the fact that I myself had experienced this disease in an earlier epidemic in the summer of 1946 was common knowledge among the group, and I believe I was evidence that the outcome need not be negative.

From the beginning, Lou impressed me as someone who, though desperately ill, sincerely believed that he would be able to return to his professional life and his beloved hobby of golf. Even as the disease progressed so that he became completely paralyzed and had to enter an iron lung respirator, he continued to be positive in his outlook. The iron lung's collar, made of sponge rubber through which one's head protruded, resulted in a certain amount of congestion, which in Lou's case was particularly prominent about his ears. He was frequently referred to—and indeed, called himself—"Louie Blue Ears," reflecting early on his ability to maintain his humor, his equanimity, and his spirit, no matter what the circumstances.

At our first meeting, I was also terribly impressed by his wife, Dottie, who was sensitive yet realistic as to the seriousness of the illness and its possible implications. I also recall his mother and father and his uncle, the closeness of the family, and the strength that he derived from all of them. As a young physician, it seemed evident to me that individuals with a comparable degree of illness reacted very differently. Not only did their personal strength influence this reaction, but also the strength they received from their immediate families. As time progressed, it was clear to them that the family would play a major role in their recovery and in their ability to function, irrespective of the magnitude of their disability.

Lou Sternburg's disability is the most profound that I have ever seen or known about in a patient who continued not just to survive but to function. Every voluntary muscle in his body is paralyzed. He can only speak by swallowing air, a process called "frog breathing," or by lying on a rocking bed, which passively moves the diaphragm and forces air in and out, allowing the use of the vocal cords. Despite this, one can carry on a conversation with him on virtually any subject. Even now, it is almost impossible for this physician to appreciate fully that this sensitive and sensible human being has not only survived but has greatly influenced all who know him. This is the result not only of his incredible inner strength but also of the equally remarkable commitment and resourcefulness of Dottie. Together, they raised two children who now have their own careers and an understanding and meaningful relationship with both parents. Through the interest of members of his community, Lou was able to manage a business from his rocking bed, and this gave him increasing confidence that he could do whatever needed to be done and whatever was of interest to him.

He thus proceeded to obtain a master's and then a doctorate degree. And he and Dottie together were able to interact successfully in social situations—at home, in the beginning, and later away from home. When my wife and I were married some three-and-a-half years after the onset of Lou's illness, we stopped by to visit the Sternburgs before beginning our honeymoon. Twenty-five years later, when our children gave us an anniversary celebration, Lou and Dottie joined us in our home.

This foreword is based upon my personal recollections and heartfelt admiration for Lou and Dottie, for their immediate family, and for their friends, who have made this remarkable story even a possibility. As I write, I have not yet read the book, because I did not wish my remarks to be influenced by its content. I need, therefore, to add one other thought— namely, the difficulty that Lou and Dottie experienced in meeting Lou's many unusual medical needs. Any physician would be hard pressed to understand the medical problems unique to someone who had had no movement of a voluntary muscle for thirty years. There have been, of course, dedicated physicians wishing to be helpful and, indeed, being helpful, but quite often the Sternburgs themselves had to guide these physicians in their clinical judgments and recommendations because the two of them obviously knew the patient better than any physician ever could.

It has been a personal privilege to know the Sternburgs, and my greatest difficulty is in finding some way to transmit to those of you privileged to read their book the strength and uniqueness of the authors. There are many examples of incredible human will recorded in history, but I am doubtful that there are any that have exceeded that of Lou Sternburg.

K. Frank Austen, M.D.

Theodore B. Bayles
Professor of Medicine, Harvard Medical School
Chairman, Department of Rheumatology and Immunology,
Brigham Women's Hospital

View from the Seesaw

one

"Is it going to rain?" From inside the tent, Susie looked anxiously out at the darkening clouds and the trees blowing in the cold wind.

"It *is* raining," I said.

"Not on my father's graduation. I can't bear it."

But she was smiling and excited. We all were. It was the day for which I had worked and wrestled and labored for so long, the day I was going to get my Ph.D. from Brandeis University. Nothing else mattered.

All the family were there—my grown-up son and daughter, my wife, her father, my mother, and my beloved Uncle Hy, who had taught me and scolded me and loved me and never let me get away with anything. The tent was on the front lawn of our house in Newton because there was going to be a great celebration party that evening. We had gathered in it to have our pictures taken. I wore the mortarboard and the black doctoral gown with three velvet bands on the wide sleeves. It was silk, very heavy and full, and long enough to cover me completely, right over my feet.

Everyone put raincoats over their best clothes, and Dottie and our children and I went in one car, and our friend A.J. drove the others. Dottie and Susie were wild with excitement. David was worrying about his camera. I had been talking about this day for weeks, but now I didn't want to talk. I wanted to think.

The ceremonies were in the Brandeis amphitheater, with the candidates on chairs in the flat space below the platform and the audience sitting and standing on the sloping grass sides all around. We arrived early. I was put at the end of the front row, where the Ph.D.'s would sit, and my family was near me at the side. The amphitheater filled up with a flowing sea of blue gowns and black umbrellas and beautiful, eager young men and women in mortarboards. At fifty-seven, I felt as young as they were, and I was proud to be in their company, all of us for this day setting aside the varied details and differences of our lives to celebrate the joy of learning and knowledge and ideas.

The doctorates were awarded last. It was an endless wait in the cold rain while a thousand students filed across the stage, but I was wearing layers of sweaters under my gown, and I loved hearing the names and watching the faces and the jaunty or serious or nervous or casual manner with which they met their great moment.

The Ph.D.'s were called up one by one to have a lone moment of glory on stage. I was the last.

"Louis Sternburg."

Here we go. Up the ramp, and when I reached the center of the platform, a roar of applause rose from the amphitheater. When the president of the university laid the blue hood around my shoulders, there was a great surge of movement, as the crowd of five thousand people rose to their feet.

For me. On the platform, the faculty was standing and applauding, too. Dottie was crying. I was grinning like a fool.

President Bernstein brought down the microphone from the podium and asked me if I would say something. I knew he might ask, so I was prepared enough to begin by congratulating my fellow graduates and their families and thanking Brandeis for what they had done for me. The rest was spontaneous. I wanted to thank my family who were there. Seeing the familiar, sensitive musician's face of my dear old Uncle

Hy, I had to tell the crowd what he meant to me. "Everyone should have an Uncle Hy."

They liked it. In the storm of delighted applause, I looked out from under the umbrella that the dean of the graduate school was holding over me and saw among the welcoming strangers the dark sparkling eyes of my beautiful daughter, the sweet serious smile of my son, the faces of my friends who had helped and encouraged me and had come to cheer me. I thanked them all, I thanked my mentor in the psychology department, and then I asked everyone to give thanks with me to the most important person there.

"My wife Dottie, who is pushing this wheelchair."

The crowd rose again. I could not turn to Dottie, because I am paralyzed, but she bent and kissed me, and for a moment we were alone among those five thousand people, with just the familiar accompaniment of the motor at the back of the chair, which runs the artificial respirator that keeps me breathing.

two

The last day of July 1955 was a Sunday, and I was on the golf course as usual. The only thing that was different was my game.

"For God's sake, Lou, you're spraying the ball all over the course."

Alan liked to rib me, to get me moving on Sunday mornings, but today he was right. For some reason, I couldn't control the ball.

We had been playing together every Saturday and Sunday morning for a couple of years now, challenging any takers for golf balls and lunch. He had the flamboyance, and I had the steadiness. A good team. We seldom lost.

"You'd better sharpen up your game before we go away," Alan said. Through golf, Dottie and I had become very friendly with Alan and his wife, Natalie. In a couple of weeks we were taking our first trip away together, to a golf resort in Maine.

"Don't worry. I'll wipe the floor with you up there."

I was looking forward to this trip. Dottie was recovering from the recent birth of our second child, Susan, a beautiful healthy girl. With David all over the place at two years old, life was busy at our house. Dottie and I couldn't spend much time alone anymore, and this was our first proper vacation.

I was a sales representative for a friend of mine who made woven labels for clothes. I was on the road a lot, and although I had often been to Maine, I'd never taken Dottie there. We were leaving the children with a nurse and two doting sets of grandparents. I'd have Dottie to myself, golf every day, good friends, lobsters, lots of laughs. I was longing for it.

Dottie met me at the club pool in the afternoon, and we relaxed and planned our trip. Relaxing was all I could do. I felt drained of energy, and it was a great effort to drag myself to Alan's backyard cookout for his son's sixth birthday. I was very sociable and lively in those days. I usually enjoyed any kind of party, but that night we went home early.

I felt rotten the next day, and by Tuesday I had started to feel very sick. I was visiting customers in Boston, so I stopped off at my father's office to rest.

He told me I looked as bad as I felt. "Better go and see Uncle Duke, Lou."

Uncle Duke was an old and very dear family friend who was a surgeon, but we went to him for everything. He was very busy, but as always he told me to "Come right over," as if I were the only patient in the world.

After listening to my lungs and giving me some bending and flexing tests for stiffness in the joints, he told me to go home and rest.

"Nothing serious. Probably just a bad cold. Let me know how you feel."

I went home, put a large pitcher of juice on the night table and crept into bed to sleep it away. This had always been my system for beating a cold and fever.

David was running around making his usual noise, so I told Dottie to take him out somewhere. "I've got to sleep, I'm exhausted."

When they came home in the late afternoon, I was worse. Dottie was scared. I'd never been sick since she had known me. I was an athlete—golf, tennis, swimming, school football hero—strong and healthy.

She called Uncle Duke. "What do I do?"

"Better have a medical man look at him."

It was the day of house calls. When Dr. Abrams came that evening, he did the same flexing tests and agreed that it must be a severe virus. He gave me an antibiotic and told Dottie to call him right away if I had any unusual symptoms.

"Like what?"

"Nausea, vomiting, headache, anything new."

I tried to drink juice, take pills, lie down and sleep, but my body had started to ache unbearably. I couldn't get comfortable. My joints ached, my arms and legs were heavy with pain, and I began to vomit. I had never felt so ill. I couldn't lie down or sit still. I paced the room like a caged animal.

At 3:30 A.M., Dottie called Dr. Abrams to tell him I was much worse and couldn't keep the pills down.

"He'll be my first house call in the morning."

She hung up, furious. "Call me right away if there's a change," he had said. Well, there sure was a change. I had all the new symptoms, so why wasn't he coming now?

Three hours later, I was so ill that she called him again. This time he came at once. He took one look at me and said, "Get dressed. You're going to a Boston hospital."

"Why?"

"For tests. We've got to get a definite diagnosis."

Of *what*? Dottie wanted to ask, but she was afraid. I was too sick to give a damn. I didn't care what they did or where they did it. I just wanted to throw my aching body down somewhere and be left alone to sleep and sleep.

Dr. Abrams started to call an ambulance to take me to Massachusetts General Hospital, but Dottie asked if she could drive me. We lived in an apartment complex, and she didn't want to scare the neighbors with the sight of an ambulance.

"Do you know how to get there?"

"I'll drive," I said feebly. "I know the way." Big hero.

"Then you show her," the doctor said.

At the hospital, they were expecting me. Dottie left me off at the main entrance and went to park the car. I walked through the swinging doors to the emergency room and gave my name to the nurse at the desk.

"Go and sit in that wheelchair, Mr. Sternburg."

She was busy with my admission form and didn't look up as I walked the few yards to the chair and sat down. Too bad. Someone should have watched me take the last steps I would ever take in my life.

In the depressing windowless waiting room, I sat miserably alone, watching the nurses and doctors crisscrossing the black and white floor tiles, appearing and disappearing through passages on their mysterious business. On dark wooden benches that looked like church pews, people of all ages sat resignedly, like passengers at a bus station, waiting to be called. None of us looked at each other.

My head was splitting. My body ached so badly I could hardly sit in the chair. I didn't know what they were going to do with me. Why was I here? What did Dr. Abrams know that he hadn't told us? I wanted to get up, get angry with someone and make them see me, but the nurse had told me to stay in the chair, so I did.

When Dottie hurried in, I got angry with her.

"How are you doing, Louis?"

"How do you think? I have a hell of a headache, I ache from head to toe, and no one's been near me. God dammit, get someone to see me soon. I'm burning up. She said I have to stay in the chair, so push me over to that water bubbler."

It was too high for me to reach from the chair. Dottie had to push me over to the one for children. I drank like a child, greedily, messily. The water was cool, but it didn't quench my thirst.

At last, an intern came and told us they were going to do a lumbar puncture. As he wheeled me away, Dottie began to come with us, but he told her to wait in the visitors' room until it was over.

On the black leather examining table, I caught an unnerving

7

glimpse of the long thin needle that was to invade my body. When they curled me up in a fetal position to expose my spine, my muscles began to twitch violently. Dr. Lassiter kept telling me to keep my body rigid, but I couldn't. I was embarrassed and humiliated. It's my nature to want to go along with what's expected of me and to try to do everything right, including spinal taps if necessary, but I couldn't control my body.

I sweated. They sweated. People walked in and out of the room and muttered to each other. You could feel the tension. They brought in new orderlies to help hold me still. They tried to relax me and talk me into calmness, but I was in a nightmare of agony, nailed to the black leather torture table, with every muscle out of control. It took three tries and more than two hours to draw out enough of the vital clear spinal fluid for analysis.

When it was over at last, I lay exhausted and twitching. I waited for Dottie, but she didn't come because they had forgotten to tell her. So she wasn't with me when the doctor came back into the small room.

I was lying on my side as they had left me after the spinal, with my head on my arm, trying to relax. I turned my aching body over and looked up at him.

"I have the report from the lab, Mr. Sternburg."

The result of the spinal had been positive. The verdict was swift and shocking.

"Poliomyelitis."

During the summer of 1955, New England was going through a deadly epidemic of this highly infectious disease, which attacks the central nervous system and can, in its severest form, cause paralysis. Every summer for the last few years many parents had kept their children out of swimming pools and away from large groups of other children, terrified that they might get polio.

It was commonly called infantile paralysis, and I knew it was for children, not for a healthy man of thirty. Not for me. Other people got dreadful diseases, had accidents, died. I lived a charmed life. I didn't have bad luck.

"Not me," I told the doctor.

"I'm afraid so, but it's diagnosed as a mild case. Nonparalytic."

Well, of course. If I had to be one of the thousands caught up in the polio epidemic, I would have the mildest version of it. My luck still held.

When Dottie came up to my bright, sunny room, where the curtains blew in a fresh breeze from the window, she was surprised to find me sitting up in bed, eating fruit salad.

"Oh, Lou, they said . . . What a relief. You don't look so bad. I was terrified."

"So was I." I kissed her, a stupid thing to do. "Thank God, it's only a mild case. Nonparalytic polio, that's not so bad. I think people get over it quite quickly. Probably a week in the hospital, and then I can go home."

To get a private room, I had to be admitted under a staff doctor, and Dr. Abrams had recommended a Dr. Vincent Perlo. When he came in, a small, mild, balding man, we weren't very impressed. He was matter-of-fact and rather aloof, and when I joked with him, because I was nervous, he didn't respond.

He examined me briefly and told me to rest. He didn't seem concerned, but when he took Dottie out into the hall, he told her, "The next seventy-two hours are critical."

"But I thought . . . " She stared at his grave face.

He shook his head. "We'll have to watch him very closely. Do you have young children at home?"

He told her to take the whole family, including Susie's nurse, to get gamma globulin shots right away.

"And I want you to stay away from the children if you're going to come to the hospital every day."

"But I can't. I have a new baby. She can't be completely separated from her mother."

"Better than having polio," Dr. Perlo said dryly.

"I don't have polio."

"It's a highly infectious virus. You could be incubating it without knowing it."

Dottie was shaken. If it was only a mild case, why was he treating it like a dangerous crisis? He had even turned the water off with his elbows when he washed his hands. How did we get stuck with him out of all the doctors on the staff? This guy was a real crepe hanger.

"He says we should all get preventive shots. It's just routine." She hid her anxiety from me. "So I'll have to go home now and take the kids to Dr. Berenberg."

We still didn't know that we shouldn't kiss good-night.

"Don't worry, Dottie."

"I won't."

Worry came later.

When she called our pediatrician, she was surprised to find he had already heard the news, and she could tell by the tremor in his voice that he was very upset. He had always given us confidence, he had kept us calm when David was born prematurely and had to be in an incubator for three weeks, but now he was different.

"Bring the children right in, and I'll take you as soon as you get here."

That was when it started. That was when the panic of the polio epidemic turned on us. The doctor didn't want Dottie and the children in the waiting room with his other patients. At home, after the news spread, which it did as rapidly as all bad news, Dottie began to find that neighborhood parents didn't want our children near theirs. I don't blame them. What would we have done? I found out years later that, because I'd been at the golf club that Sunday, they emptied the pool and closed the dining room. The Sternburg family were lepers.

The next morning when I tried to sit up, I tumbled backward in bed. I had never lost control of my body before. What the hell was happening to me?

When Dr. Perlo came in, I was breathing more rapidly. He listened to my chest and had me move my arms and legs, but in his usual noncommittal way he showed no sign of finding anything unusual.

He felt my throat. "Any trouble swallowing?"

"Breakfast went down all right."

He nodded and left. When he came back, he looked more worried. "There's some weakness in your chest muscles. I'm transferring you to White Twelve, a floor just for infectious diseases. They'll put you into a respirator to ease your breathing and make you more comfortable."

The trip to the other end of the hospital was swift, but the hot humid air pressed like a weight on my chest. In a corner room, shades were drawn to keep out the hot August sun, and in the dim light I could see a long yellow cylinder open to show a sheeted mattress.

What the hell was this? Dr. Perlo's "respirator" looked more like an iron lung. I thought about Fred Snite, the Miami Beach playboy who was famous for having lived helplessly in his iron lung for twenty years. We'd seen him on movie newsreels. But he had serious paralytic polio. I didn't. I had a little "chest weakness." You didn't put a man in an iron lung just for that.

Apparently you did. With a great deal of fuss and commotion, two nurses and an orderly lifted me onto the slab mattress and pushed me into the iron lung. They clamped the tank shut, and although I could hear the pump working, it didn't affect my breathing. The nurses hastily tightened

11

the rubber collar around my neck to keep air from escaping, so that the tank would expand and contract my lungs. What the hell was going on? I'd been getting enough air, but they behaved as if I were about to suffocate.

My head was outside the iron lung, and I was staring into a mirror above my face, which reflected the confusion. I could see that the nurses were very watchful and anxious. If I had known then that I was the first patient to be put into an iron lung respirator at Massachusetts General, I would have been even more anxious than they were.

I was restless and on edge. My temperature had been rising steadily, and although the respirator had a small air conditioner inside, it was claustrophobic. My broad shoulders knocked against the sides every time I moved.

To keep me occupied, my nurse, Miss Oates, pushed me over to the window for a reverse view in the mirror attached to the top of the tank. She raised the shade so I could watch the trains below in the switching yard, backing and shunting, moving slowly away toward the river, sparkling in the noonday sun. The view from the twelfth floor brought back memories of the model train set I had when I was a happy child in the third floor flat of a house opposite Franklin Park, where my grandmother, sitting on the porch with me, would watch the baseball and tell me Yiddish tales from Poland.

I had always loved trains because they promised adventure in faraway places. I closed my eyes now and let a train carry me away from all this. Away from the iron lung, from fever, from polio, I floated through space for what seemed a long time.

"Louis."

I woke up. In the mirror, I saw Dottie's eyes, huge and anxious over a hospital mask. The shock of seeing me in an iron lung had caused her bright skin to pale. When Dr. Perlo called to tell her that I was in a respirator, she had pictured an oxygen tent over the bed, like in the movies.

She tried to hide her shock with jokes about the mask and the long green hospital gown that everyone had to wear on the isolation floor. She began to prattle, about the kids, about the family, about the trains below the window, anything to cover her distress. When I asked her to get me a candy bar, she was glad of the chance to get out of the room and regain her composure.

Restless with fever, I had been moving around in my iron prison quite easily, but by the time Dottie came back, I was having some trouble with my left leg. I couldn't lift it off the mattress.

She saw the look on my face. "What's wrong?"

"Little trouble lifting my left leg," I said casually. "Just a cramp."

Her face froze. We each knew what the other was thinking, but neither of us could say it.

Paralysis.

"Shall I call the nurse?" she whispered.

"No," I whispered back. "It'll go away."

"Of course it will."

We whispered to each other, her face close to mine. We could make it not be true.

"Take it easy, Lou. Relax. Don't get upset."

She looked so upset herself that I managed to say lightly, "I'm not going to let a little thing like this ruin my golf game. Not after I finally shot a seventy-one last week."

She laughed—and what a blessing her laughter was! Her beautiful blue-gray eyes with long curling lashes had a steady, luminous depth above the mask. I knew my wife's physical beauty and the strong spirit behind it, but now I saw for the first time something indomitable.

Through the mask, she kissed my forehead. I silently prayed

13

that this nightmare would end, so that I could go home with this lovely, loving woman and resume our life together.

I dozed a bit, and when I woke, I tried to move my left leg again. It was a lead weight. All right, I'll move my right leg. Nothing. An icy fear went through me. I tried again. My right leg was also paralyzed.

I was swept by a terror unlike anything I had ever known. What about my arms? I was afraid to try them. Look, God, I'm a healthy, independent young man, active, vital, with a wife and kids to take care of, a life to live, a thousand things I have to do. Listen, God—please, God, don't take my arms away!

Somehow I got the courage to try them. They wouldn't move. My whole body was paralyzed.

"Nurse!" I cried out. "Something's wrong. I can't move— help me!"

I heard the nurse rushing over to me. Then a new wave of terror seized me as I suddenly lost my breath. She had opened a porthole in the side of the respirator, and I was suffocating. I screamed for help, but it came out only as a faint whisper.

"Help me! Somebody please help me—please . . . "

At last she closed the porthole. I was gasping and choking.

"Just breathe with the machine," she said coolly. "Don't fight it."

"Easy for you to say . . . you bitch." I could hardly speak. "You're out there—breathing." I gasped and coughed. "I'm in here. Don't open that damn door again."

Miss Oates looked at me impassively. Then her face disappeared from the mirror.

My eyes filled with tears of rage and self-pity. They had lied to me. This wasn't a mild case of polio. I was deathly sick, paralyzed, trapped in this steel cage, my body stiff and lifeless.

My mind felt paralyzed, too. I could only think, "Why me? What did I ever do to deserve this? Not me, please, not me."

14

Dottie's face came into the mirror. "Not me!" I begged silently. My eyes pleaded tearfully with her anguished eyes for her to save me, but she couldn't. No one could. I was lost.

"Don't open that door again," she told the nurse breathlessly. "He can't stand it."

Dottie's brother had died a horrible struggling death from cancer two years earlier, and she couldn't forget how callous some of the nurses had been.

"I know what I'm doing," Miss Oates told her sharply.

Actually, she did. She was a trained polio nurse who had been flown in from Chicago during this epidemic, but she was cold and detached, and Dottie didn't trust her at all. Things were getting out of hand. I was going downhill in front of her eyes, and something had to be done.

"I'm going to call the doctor, Lou." She threw me a distracted kiss and ran from the room. I heard her footsteps fading down the hall and the whine of the descending elevator. I didn't know when she would come back. I couldn't see the nurse in the mirror. I didn't know where she was. I was helpless and alone.

three

The next day, Dr. Perlo called Uncle Duke to tell him how I was.

"It's reached the fourth vertebra," he said. "It's now in the hands of God."

My fever had taken a sudden jump, and I drifted into delirium. I felt euphoric, weightless, and free of the forces of gravity in a long hallucinatory dream. The next elevator I thought I heard was in an aircraft carrier in the Pacific during World War II. I was standing next to an officer with gold braid on his hat. We were going down to the mess hall. I walked through the cafeteria line and took scrambled eggs and fruit, and as I sat down, I recognized the face of the man next to me. What was my golf idol Ben Hogan doing on this ship, out of uniform and wearing his famous gray cardigan and white cap? We were surrounded by a surrealistic fog, as if we were in a Fellini film.

Lapsing in and out of comas, I didn't know day from night, real from unreal, but I was aware of agonizing pain and the constant invasion of my aching body by needles and tubes.

By the third day, so much fluid had built up in my lungs that I wasn't getting enough oxygen. I was drowning in my own secretions. My mind was a whirling eddy of flashing colors and strange clouded visions. I floated free of my body, and I guess I was pretty near death. When I started to turn blue, the doctors had to do an emergency tracheotomy to save my life. I came back to earth to see in the mirror a metal tube in the base of my neck. It made it possible to suck out secretions before I suffocated again.

A few days later, with my fever subsiding, I began to be vaguely aware of where I was. Turning my head, I could see another iron lung in the dimly lit room. My mind was dusky, but I guessed there was a patient inside, since the brown leather bellows were pumping rhythmically in and out.

With air escaping through the hole in my neck, it was almost impossible to speak. Hoarsely and feebly, I tried to shout.

"How are you doing?" No answer. With all the strength I could gather, I yelled again. Still no answer.

Miss Oates appeared next to my head. "Did you call?"

My God, somebody *had* heard me. Miss Oates, who was a bitch, seemed suddenly like Florence Nightingale.

"Are you all right? Is there anything I can do?"

"Yeah, get me out of this thing and give me my walking papers."

She laughed without mirth.

"Who's in the other lung?"

"A nice young man named David. I'm looking after both of you."

"Say hello to him for me. Tell him my son's name is David, too."

Dave's voice was louder than mine. We tried to talk, but we couldn't synchronize our speech to compete with the loud rhythmic whooshing of the bellows. We both needed a lot of care and vied constantly for the nurse's attention, especially when the nurse was gorgeous red-haired Sally, who was a welcome relief from the austere Miss Oates. I called her all the time, whether I needed her or not.

David's parents were there every day. They looked old enough to be his grandparents, quiet and controlled, with a

17

sort of grim stillness like the people in the Grant Wood painting where the man looks as if he might go berserk some day and attack his wife with the pitchfork.

Dave was doing much better than I was. That wasn't difficult. Anyone who wasn't actually dying was in better shape than me. I knew him only by his voice. I never saw him, but he was fictionalized in my mind as about nineteen, tall, dark, and good-looking, and I built up an unreasonable jealousy because I thought he had all the luck.

Uncle Duke wouldn't let my mother come because she was supposed to be too frail to bear the sight of me in the iron lung. She had always been overprotected and subservient to her husband, although actually she was as strong as anyone, and it would have been much easier for her to be with me and know what was going on. My father took six weeks off from work and came with Dottie every day. She was staying with my parents near the hospital. Some of our friends, like Alan and Natalie, ignored the risk of infection and went to see the children, because Dottie couldn't, and gave her news of them every day. They bought food, cleaned the house, and brought Dottie the mail and silly stories of what David had said and remarkable feats performed by the baby. They were marvelous.

My dad had to wear a hospital cap and gown and a mask over his face, but in his eyes I saw anguish. He was a successful businessman with a lot of influence around Boston, and for the first time in his life he had run into something he couldn't control.

He groped desperately for some way to help me. He brought candy to the nurses so they would be nice to me. He befriended the doctors for the same reason. He fed me and shaved me and talked to me endlessly about our old days together. I had been his little prince, and we would walk in the park after dinner and discuss business and baseball and world events, as if we were the same age.

My dad was the most important man in my life. He was my best friend. He was a short, round, bald, jolly man, much loved for his wit and honesty and invigorating optimism. But now his only son had polio and couldn't move. As I got worse and his confidence weakened, this hopeful, cheerful man became sad and bitter.

Although she was only twenty-five, Dottie became the stronger one. Up to this time, she had been rather quiet and shy. She hadn't had to cope with anything; I had been in charge. But, faced with this crisis of a paralyzed husband who might die, she began to show some of the incredible strength and resourcefulness that were to be my best hope for survival.

She protected me like a tigress, constantly watching the nurses and doctors. When her brother was dying, she had been terribly distressed to see how inhumanely he was treated, more like an object than a suffering person. She wasn't going to let this happen to me. She decided who were the best doctors and wouldn't let anyone else near me. She learned how to help the overworked nurses by doing as much as she could for me herself. No one got away with anything. Once when she saw a young nurse leave two iron lung patients alone to go out and talk to her boyfriend, Dottie went after her and brought her back.

In spite of my helpless situation, she was still very desirable to me. Her blue-gray eyes tantalized me. I wanted to be out of this iron lung and away from the hospital, just alone with her. I couldn't move, but I could feel—incredible feelings of passion. Along with all the infections, I had erections. Good old Lou, paralyzed, but still preoccupied with sex.

I was getting better. My fever went down. They put a reverse vacuum cleaner on top of the lung to blow extra air into me when my ear lobes looked too blue.

Dr. Frank Austen, a resident who was head of the polio

team, had had polio himself at college, and he used to come and give me pep talks when I couldn't sleep at night.

"I made it, and so can you, Louie Blue Ears. You've got the guts for it."

One day I wiggled my toes, only slightly, but all the staff on the floor came in to cheer. Then I began to be able to swallow. I was on my way.

But each time I made progress, something came in from left field and smashed me. All at once, I was choking. The lung was breathing me, but I couldn't breathe. They had to do a bronchoscopy in the middle of the night, a horrible procedure like sword swallowing that involved a tube down my throat to suction up the suffocating mucus until I could breathe again. It was agony, and I had to suffer through it at least once a week.

One of the fears of those days, a fear that still haunts me thirty years later, was of losing electric power. This started when a hurricane threatened to hit Boston. There was a panic about whether the emergency generators could keep sixty respirators going, as well as the rest of the hospital load. The storm didn't hit, but the dread of it showed me how totally dependent I was on the hated machine.

Night and day, I longed to be released from the iron lung. The polio team tried turning it off to see if I could breathe at all without it. I couldn't. I wished they hadn't tried, so I could still imagine I didn't need it.

When they turned it on again and I could speak feebly, I said, "My toes came back. Why not my lungs?"

"Be patient," they told me, but I was frustrated and miserable. Toes were one thing. I wanted to breathe by myself *now*.

The polio epidemic, which was the last serious one before Salk vaccine mercifully made them obsolete, had caught Massachusetts General Hospital off guard. Up until then, Children's Hospital in Boston had taken in any adult patients, but that summer of 1955 there were too many of us, and we had to go to hospitals that were not experienced or properly equipped.

At Mass. General, there weren't enough nurses for the iron lung patients, so they moved us all to a special unit on the ninth floor—sixty iron lungs head to toe in a chaos of machinery, cables, thunderous bellows, extra lungs out in the corridor, nurses scurrying about, anxious families, visitors tripping over the cables, doctors dealing with crisis after crisis of choking, seizures, heart failure.

Uncle Duke's wife Estelle said the scene was like a medieval pest house, complete with the stink. We were helpless, and it was impossible to keep us clean all the time.

I didn't even care. I was desperately ill again. Nurses and technicians going from patient to patient in the crowded ward carried infections, and I caught them all. My fever went up and down like an elevator. I had every medical complication except heart failure. I was one of the sickest patients there. But although others in the ward were dying all around me, for some reason—which I still don't really understand—I clung to life by a tenuous thread. And in the iron lung, it was a life of unrelenting agony.

For weeks I had spent twenty-four hours a day encased in the tank respirator. My shoulders rubbed against the steel sides, and the seventy pounds I had lost made the mattress seem thinner. I developed a severe bedsore. My airtight collar chafed back and forth with each breath just below my tracheotomy tube.

The tank was hell, but at least it was safe. When the porthole was opened, I couldn't breathe. I was like a diver without enough reserve air, struggling and gasping to reach the surface, screaming at the nurses in impotent silence in the eternity before the porthole was closed. I didn't want them to clean me up. I only wanted air.

My mother Katherine, a beautiful woman with a radiant smile, had always scoured our house like a demon and was said to be "crazy clean." She passed some of this on to me, and I've always been a bit obsessive. As a small child, my worst nightmare was to commit the vile sin of messing my pants. But now I lay in filth, uncaring. At first, the only thing that mattered was keeping me alive. As I slid in and out of comas, the nurses stuffed wadding around me and the lung got more and more insanitary. I could feel wet and dirty, but as my head was outside the lung, I couldn't smell much.

The harried nurses had to try to clean us up periodically, because of the bedsores. Dr. Norm Anderson, the polio team's anesthesiologist, brought oxygen equipment and kept me alive by "bag breathing" while I was being washed.

After he attached the oxygen line to my tracheotomy tube, the nurses went into a frenzy of activity to get done as soon as possible. They pulled the slab with the mattress out of the lung, and he breathed me by rhythmically squeezing a bag on the oxygen line, as he would do to help a patient's breathing during an operation, forcing air into my lungs through the tracheotomy tube.

Out of the lung, I was helpless, dependent on the hands and skill of the artificial breather to keep my air coming. I always panicked. I was sure I would die. They probably had to use more wadding when I was out of the lung than when I was in it.

To clean me up, they had to roll me on my side. That made me deathly afraid. Suppose the breathing tube didn't turn with me? I was disoriented by being turned, and the dizziness intensified the panic. I was caught in a maelstrom, a violent bottomless whirlpool of terror sucking me down into a helpless vertigo so powerful that I still shiver when I think about it now.

I hated being bag-breathed, and I hated being cleaned up.

The Marquis de Sade couldn't have thought up a worse form of torture.

As the polio epidemic continued, there were soon too many patients to be bag-breathed while they were bathed. The polio team had to come up with another idea.

Looking belatedly at the instructions for the Emerson iron lung, they saw that a plastic bubble, something like an Air Force tail gunner's capsule, could be used for positive pressure breathing. It could be clamped over the patient's head, and as soon as the tank was open and the slab rolled out, the mechanism switched from suction and forced air into the bubble. The hospital hadn't used it yet, and they decided to try it out on me.

Unfortunately, they didn't notice one thing about the bubble. It had been in a storeroom and had not been cleaned since the day they got it. When they clamped it to the tank and the air rushed in to breathe me, it created a dust storm inside the plastic globe, and I couldn't breathe. Five people were working feverishly to bathe me. I couldn't yell out, and it was an eternity before they noticed the sandstorm. In horror, the nurses slammed shut the lung and unclamped the bubble.

Of all the terrors I'd been through in the hospital, this was the worst. I thought I was gone—me, a World War II sailor, gasping for his life in the sand. I coughed for hours.

They never used the bubble on me again at Mass. General. It was back to the dreaded bag breathing, and my slow, sick life went on.

Dottie When Lou went into Mass. General and we found out he had polio, my first reaction was disbelief. This couldn't be happening to us. This was the first crisis of our marriage. Up to then, everything in our life had been beautiful. I had married the man I loved, we had two healthy children and a lot of friends and fun, and my greatest worry was what to wear to a party or what to cook for dinner.

Our parents had always made things easy for us. If something went wrong, they could fix it. So when this terrible thing happened to us, I knew that my father-in-law would know who to call and what to do to make it all better.

The day they put Lou in the iron lung was like a bad dream, and I went back to his family's house for dinner in a state of shock. My parents were there and Uncle Duke and Estelle. Ever since Lou's mother's mastectomy twelve years before, she had always been protected from anything nasty. When Dr. Perlo called me that morning to say Lou was on the danger list, I hadn't been able to tell her. How could I tell her now that he was in an iron lung and couldn't move his arms and legs?

They thought my dazed look was tiredness, and my mother told me to go upstairs and rest. I was glad not to have to answer questions yet. When I had rushed out of Lou's room and called Dr. Perlo, he kept repeating, "I can't minimize the seriousness of the situation. I have to tell you, Mrs. Sternburg, I cannot minimize the seriousness of the situation."

That was all I could hear. I had known we were not immune to disaster because of my brother's death, but I had never thought lightning could strike twice in the same family. Now I knew it could, and I had to get Lou's father alone to tell him the trouble we were in, so he could start fixing it right away.

When I heard him on the stairs, I called to him. He came into my room, and I told him what had happened, so that he could jump into action. Instead, this poor man, who loved his son more than anything in the world, just sat there on the bed dazed and asked me, "What are we going to do?"

He was asking *me*. If it's possible to grow up in an instant,

I think I did it then. I realized that I would have to be responsible not only for myself, but for decisions that could affect Lou's life. It was here. It was real, and I had to face it. No one was going to make this all better for me.

Next day at the hospital, Lou's father suddenly seemed much older. I had known him as a cheery, confident man who was on top of any situation as soon as he came into the room. Now as he stood by the iron lung, gazing wretchedly at the face that was all he could see of his son, he looked as if all the wind were knocked out of him. He fumbled for words. He stammered when he spoke to the nurse. When it was time to go, he pulled off his glasses as he took off his mask, and they smashed on the floor.

"It's all right, I'll drive." I bent to pick up the broken lenses.

"You won't." It was the last straw. "I can drive my own car."

We had a fight about it, going out of the hospital to the car park. I had never dared to argue with him before, but I wasn't going to be driven home by a man in his emotional state who couldn't even see.

I won. I drove home. I had grown up.

Growing strong wasn't something I made myself do. It happened. This is the way it is when you're suddenly caught up in a crisis.

In those weeks at Mass. General, people sometimes said to me, "I don't know how you do it." They still say it.

"If it happened to you," I always answer, "you'd do it too."

You do whatever has to be done. There's nothing else to do.

I had a wonderful husband whom I admired and adored. I had idolized my brother, and I lost him. I was damned if this terrible virus was going to take my husband away from me, too. If he died, I saw myself as a depressing young widow with two small children and very little money. In 1955, it was harder for women to get jobs. I would probably have to give up Boston, which I loved, and go back to my family's home in Framingham, the small slow town I thought I had left for ever.

If Lou died, I would never get over it. I needed him desperately, and I clung to the belief that if he lived, he would recover completely.

So I began my crusade. I did anything I could to help. The nurses were overwhelmed, so I rolled up my sleeves and learned how to give alcohol and ice rubdowns to bring down Lou's temperature. I emptied catheters, ran for supplies, applied hot packs to alleviate the pain of muscle spasm, anything they would let me do.

When mucus got caught in Lou's windpipe and he would turn red and start to choke, I always thought it was the end. He couldn't call the nurse, and she couldn't keep a constant eye on both him and David, so I had to watch Lou all the time and call for help if it was something I couldn't cope with. When the nurse was busy with Lou and David needed something, he would call, "Nurse! Nurse! . . . Dottie!"

As a child, I never wanted to be a nurse like most girls, but here I was. I learned about vital signs and what the blood tests meant and what was serious and what wasn't. I spent most of my waking hours at the hospital. When I wasn't there, I shuddered every time the phone rang and rehearsed in my mind what I would hear. "I'm sorry, Mrs. Sternburg . . . "

Alone or with my father-in-law, I would get off the elevator each morning with a gnawing in my gut, afraid to see what new crisis was going on. On the third day, I turned the corner and saw half a dozen doctors and nurses scurrying in and out of Lou's room. One of the interns had just done an emergency tracheotomy. I had never heard the word before, let alone seen someone with a metal tube sticking out of his neck. There was blood everywhere. They were still swabbing it up. Lou's eyes looked at mine in the mirror, pleading, victimized. He couldn't speak, because the exhaled air came out of the tube, not his mouth.

Another morning, the elevator door opened on Lou's familiar iron lung in the hallway, without him in it. It was like the riderless horse at the funeral of the fallen chief, with the stirrups and boots turned backwards.

"Oh God, he's gone—and I wasn't here!"

I rushed to the room without stopping to put on the gown and mask. He was there, still alive in another lung. The air conditioner on the old one had cracked and leaked cold water over him.

When he was in the big ward with the other patients, people were dying every day. All the families got off the elevator with the same sinking feeling: who's next? As I got to know them, with the quick friendships of crisis, there was that wrench: thank God, it's not Lou. But oh, poor Joe—it's his wife.

It seemed like a game of chance. Someone you thought wasn't very sick would be gone the next day, and Lou, who was sicker than most, was hanging on. He was in agony with muscle spasms, his temperature was raging, and he went in and out of comas, but occasionally he was lucid. He would crack a joke like his old self, and for a moment the tension was relieved.

The days spread into weeks and months. Time blurred. I didn't see my friends, and although I was allowed to go home to my children after the first month, I could only be with them a short time in the mornings before I went off to the hospital until late at night. I worried about David, who had been used to having me all to himself. Now he had a new baby sister, no father, and only part of a mother, but, thank goodness, the baby's nurse gave him as much attention as the baby.

Poor woman, she had all her other jobs cancelled because people were terrified of polio infection, so she stayed on, ostracized by the world. Her sister, who had four children, wouldn't let her go there on her day off, so she just took care of our children seven days a week for months. I felt terrible for her and glad of her at the same time.

The families of the other polio patients became my family, because we shared a common catastrophe. The hospital became my world. My life had only one purpose—to keep this man I loved alive. I grew thinner and thinner. My skin lost its color. Every day was tense with anxiety, and at night I dreamed that the intravenous had become clogged, or Lou's temperature had shot up and he was delirious, or that they had to draw blood for critical tests, and I wasn't there to hold his arm.

Sometimes I dreamed that he had died, and I woke crying and stifled my sobs under the bedclothes, because it upset Lou's parents if I broke down.

Next morning, I would hurry to the ward to make sure Lou hadn't slipped away from me. Death was stalking us. I mustn't let up my guard.

The original team of interns and residents stayed on the floor for an extra month because of the epidemic. By the time they left, we had become very close. They had worked devotedly, sometimes almost twenty-four hours a day for three or four days.

The good-byes in the ward were sad. Frank Austen saved me for the last. As I was leaving for the night, he came to me and told me that he would always be our friend, which he still is.

"Keep your spirits up. You've got the guts for it," he said, which was what he was always telling Lou. "Even though Lou will probably always need mechanical assistance to breathe . . . "

I didn't hear the rest of the sentence. I kissed him good-bye, ran to the elevator, went out to the parking lot, and sat in my car and bawled like a baby.

He was wrong, he must be wrong. No one had told me anything like this. The nurses said optimistic things like, "Look, he can wiggle his toes, and they're the farthest from the brain." I didn't tell anyone what Frank had said. I was trying to make it not be true, but I had been given my first suspicion of what the future might hold.

four

"Good morning, Louis." A white coat appeared in the mirror over my iron lung. "I'm Dr. Ferris. How do you feel today?"

"Lousy. I can't seem to get ahead of these infections. I've been here three months, and I'm still picking up everything in this hell hole. I'll never get out."

Following the white coat upward, I saw a lanky athletic man, his balding head still tanned from the summer sun. He was the Children's Hospital and Harvard Medical School consultant to this polio ward.

"We want to get you out. How would you like to be transferred to a rehabilitation hospital?"

"Transferred? How am I going any place in this thing?"

"Leave that to us. You get yourself stabilized, and we'll get you on your way."

I looked up at him, my heart racing. This was the first genuine glimmer of hope I'd had from any doctor. Rehabilitation meant I'd learn to walk again. If I could have breathed faster than the machine, I would have.

But I was in a Catch-22 cycle. As long as I kept getting infections, I couldn't be moved, and if I wasn't moved from this crowded ward, I would keep on getting infections.

Dottie I went to see the small hospital in Wellesley, which had once been a convalescent home for Children's Hospital and was now partly converted to a unit for polio patients. It was called the Mary MacArthur Respiratory Center, in memory of Helen Hayes's daughter, who had died of polio when she was at Wellesley College.

I was very impressed by the place. The emphasis was on getting patients ready to go home, whereas at Mass. General it was just keeping them alive from day to day. Mary MacArthur was more like a home than a hospital. There were enough experienced staff for the patients, and I even saw a nurse brushing the long hair of a woman in an iron lung, an unheard-of luxury at Mass. General, unless the family did it.

There were only eight places for adults with respiratory polio, but because of the epidemic, there were about two hundred people waiting for them. Our only worry was whether Lou would get in. We had set our hearts on it. It would be the start of his coming home, and in both our minds coming home meant walking home.

Dr. Perlo agreed that Lou should go, even though he would be looked after by Children's Hospital doctors, not by him. He had been wonderful. He had calmed our anxieties and listened sympathetically to all our frustrations. Knowing that Lou's illness was critical, he would visit him several times a day, every day of the week. He always answered calls from me. If something was going wrong, I would call him before the staff did. He would immediately tell the polio team what to do and then come himself to check on them.

We'd been quite wrong about him. He wasn't a crepe hanger. He wasn't aloof. He was shy and quiet and confident, and utterly dependable. We had grown to respect Dr. Perlo and even to love him, but he wasn't the kind of man to whom you could say that. I don't believe we ever thanked him enough.

When Dr. Ferris got Lou a place at the Wellesley center,

the hospital staff reacted in different ways. Lou had been their first iron lung patient and perhaps the most seriously ill to survive. A lot of people had pulled together for him in the tug of war against death, and they were very proud of him. He was their star patient. Frank Austen, who had saved his life with the tracheotomy, had become a close confidant and friend. He wanted Lou to go to Wellesley, but there were some doctors who didn't, because he would be in the care of Children's Hospital, not Mass. General. I couldn't believe their attitude. I thought hospitals were only interested in getting people better, and it was a shock to discover that there were politics and jealousies here, like everywhere else.

A few days before Lou was to move, a young intern stopped me on my way into the polio ward.

"Mrs. Sternburg, can I speak to you?"

My heart sank. *My God, another crisis.* Lou had been precarious for weeks, and it seemed I had to face a new catastrophe almost every day.

The intern took me into a small room. "I understand you're planning to move your husband to Wellesley?"

"Yes, I'm very excited about it."

"Well, I'm very much against it. You've obviously no idea how serious your husband's condition is. This hospital is one of the few places in the country that can keep him alive."

"But doctors I respect have advised it. They'd never—"

"Look, you're taking him out of a general hospital with all the lifesaving facilities and putting him into a small center that doesn't even have a doctor there all the time. What if he chokes in the middle of the night? Will they know what to do?"

"Of course they will. There's a doctor there twenty-four hours a day. I've been there and talked to them. I'd trust them in an emergency."

The intern looked sternly at me. "It's my duty to tell you," he said pompously, "that by moving your husband, you'll probably kill him."

I was furious with him. "We'll prove you wrong," I muttered, and left him. How could this inexperienced ass, not long out of medical school, disagree with three distinguished doctors? Insidious doubt crept in to nag at my anger—what if he was right?—but I shook it off and went ahead with the plans.

We sometimes wonder if that pompous doctor is still around, and if he knows that Lou is too.

Miraculously, I began to build up a natural immunity to this unnatural environment, and the infections and crises that had plagued me subsided at last. By November, they were able to move me to the Mary MacArthur Center.

Outside my room, the nurses and doctors on whom I had depended for every breath were lined up to see me off.

"Good-bye, Lou."

"Good luck."

"Give 'em hell."

"Don't forget us."

Forget them! They had saved my life. Tears filled my eyes. I only just managed to say, "Thanks. I'll come . . . I'll walk back in . . . see you guys."

The elevator, which had been wired for the lung, went down so fast that my stomach was still on the ninth floor when the door opened at the basement commissary to let me out. As I rolled between the gray, steel food tables, I got glimpses in my mirror of colorful fruit and vegetables. For the first time in months, I smelled cooking. Suddenly I burst into the daylight. The sun was harsh in my eyes, and Dottie shaded them with her hand.

Parked at the loading dock was a small moving van with a

gasoline generator bolted to the floor. The orderlies pushed my lung into the cargo space and plugged it in. Dottie got in with one of the doctors and an anesthesiologist with his bag-breathing equipment—just in case—and Nurse Oates, unruffled as ever. I had been through so many traumas and crises with her that we were now friends.

As I went from the sunlight into the dark van, I could hear the truck engine running and the generator, thank God. The top half of the rear door was left open, so I could see out as we whizzed through the streets of Boston. I had been down Beacon Street and through Kenmore Square hundreds of times, but never like this. The mirrored scene behind me disappeared in blurred perspective, as if I were on a railroad observation platform, police sirens wailed, all traffic stopped, and we went through red lights, all the fifteen miles to Wellesley. I felt like a celebrity.

In the suburban gardens, I was surprised to see that the tidy lawns were pale and the leaves gone from the trees. What had happened to fall? Time had been so muddled that I hadn't realized I'd missed a whole season.

We drove between grassy slopes, stopped, and backed up to the bottom of a long cement ramp. They put a hook onto the lung and pulled me up the ramp with a winch, then pushed me into the building and plugged me in at once. I had arrived at my new home, where I was to live for almost a year. My fight for life had ended, and my fight to live had just begun.

"Welcome to Mary MacArthur, Lou. My name's Peg, and I'm the head nurse."

Our eyes met in the mirror. A bony, serious face with sandy eyebrows and lashes and steady eyes behind thick glasses. Peg looked like someone I could trust, someone who'd understand that, although I was physically well enough to be here, my spirit was still wallowing about in the uncertainties of depression and was going to need a lot of encouragement.

In a large ward with iron lungs on each side, three people transferred me quickly from one tank to the other, but I had time to see that my new lung had a plastic bubble attached, and my heart sank in dread. When I was settled, I looked in the mirror and saw that each lung across the ward had a bubble hanging from it too.

"Not me," I would tell Peg firmly. "I'm not getting in one of those things."

She came back with two orderlies to examine me and clean me up. "Have you ever been in one of these plastic shells?"

"Have I ever? I damn near choked to death. You're not getting me in that thing."

"Oh yes I am." Peg smiled. "Trust us, Lou. We know what we're doing. That's why you're here."

Peg never gave you much choice. Sometimes she would ask you, "Do you want to do such and such?" But she had already decided that you would.

My heart was in my throat as the bubble was raised and latched shut around my protruding head. As the air rushed into it, the iron lung was opened and my slab pulled out so they could get at me. My God, I was breathing! Without the dust, there didn't seem to be any special trick to it. I got dizzy when they rolled me on my side to look at my bedsore, but it was a controlled dizziness, not the terrifying vertigo I had experienced before.

They shut the lung and Peg unlatched the bubble. "You faker, you didn't seem to mind that at all."

"It was a hell of a lot better than bag breathing."

"You've got a flaming two-inch hole in your back. We've padded around it to let the air get at it, and tomorrow we'll really work on it. You relax now, and I'll show your wife around. Yell if you need me."

I knew that Peg would come at once if I did need her. Winding down from the excitement of the journey, I began to feel more at ease than at any time since polio swooped down and took away my good life.

Compared to the Mass. General polio ward, this was hospital heaven. There were enough nurses to take care of us calmly and thoroughly. The clean, uncluttered ward, flooded with light, had pale blue walls and blue cubicle curtains that Peg had drawn round my bed when she went to work on me. In the pest house, everyone could see everything that went on. We had all been Peeping Toms, forced to watch the most private details of each other's lives. It was like being in an emergency field hospital where you heard the moans of agony all around you and realized that you were part of the horror. The polio ward had been a torture chamber in Bedlam. I lay peacefully in my new lung and savored the rediscovery of privacy.

Outside the opposite window, people were moving about on the grass, their colorful clothes a welcome relief after the white nurses' uniforms and doctors' jackets that had dominated my sterile field of vision for so long. There really was a world out there where people breathed and walked and could laugh loudly.

There were four adult patients on each side of the ward, five men and three women, strangers now, but our lives would become closely entwined. We were in one wing of what had once been a beautiful country house. There was a sun porch at one end of the ward, at the other a smaller space partitioned off for children. Beyond that, a passage led to the unknown and the mysterious.

The long and difficult job of the rehab center was to prepare me to go home and live as normally as possible. At Mass. General the vital question had been, "Can we keep him alive?" Here, with less risk of infections, it was not, "Is he going to live?" but "*How* is he going to live?"

Since I half wiggled my toes at Mass. General, I had never got back any more movement, but I was convinced that as I got better, I would walk again by myself. I would start with a bar overhead, chinning myself to develop my shoulders and arms. Then I'd get my legs down and I'd stand, then walk between parallel bars, and then I'd walk out of here and go home.

At the moment, I was a wreck that had been hit by a tornado. The job of the rehab staff was to pick up the remaining debris and rebuild it bit by bit, pushing me to the limits of what I could endure. My job was to work with them and to have the mental and physical guts to try everything.

One of the first trials was a psychiatrist named Howard Blaine, who was to see me three times a week. He sat on a high stool behind me, as if my iron tank were a leather couch. I had the advantage of a mirror to see the psychiatrist, which most patients don't have as they lie and talk to an invisible listener, who may be asleep or reading or filing his nails.

"How's your sex life, Louis?" He was about my age, blond, with a classy brown tweed jacket and a slight Scandinavian accent.

"Terrific, how's yours? What kind of a dumb question is that? Are you trying to shock me? Cut out the crap, Doc."

"What do you think of what's happened to you?"

"I loved every minute. What the hell do you think I think of it?" I was furious at the idea that they thought I needed psychiatric help.

He was unmoved. "What are you thinking about?"

"Nothing."

"Do you feel sorry for yourself?"

"Well, I'm not thrilled, but I'm going to beat this rap anyway, so what's the difference?"

"I need to know how you're feeling."

"I need to be left alone. I don't have much use for shrinks."

"Well, Louis"—why couldn't I offend him?—"I just came to introduce myself. I'll be back, and I hope you'll let us get to know each other. Maybe I can be some help. You're in a tough spot."

What the hell did he know about being caged in an iron monster, whooshing away sixteen times to the minute? What could he do for me? I'd always been a fighter. I'd fight my way out of this, and I didn't need Freud to help me.

I was still steaming when Peg came to stand over me.

"Who sent the shrink?" I asked her.

"Dr. Blaine? That's routine." She smiled. "Come on, Lou, let's go for a ride."

"Where to?"

"On the rocking bed."

In my mirror, I had seen a patient across the room moving up and down in what looked like an iron rocking horse contraption.

"No."

"Let's try it."

"I get seasick on amusement park rides." You couldn't win with Peg, but you could sometimes buy time.

"We'll give you a Dramamine. Come on, the bed will breathe you better than the lung. Trust me, there's no danger. I have dozens of rocking bed alumni."

Trust? I couldn't even trust myself. Look how my own body had failed me. This damn, cursed disease, it was making a wreck out of me. Was that why they sent the man in the brown tweed jacket? I had to get myself together. I had to get out of here. "You've got the guts for it," Frank Austen had said. All right, maybe I did.

"How will that thing breathe me?" I asked cautiously.

"By the seesaw motion. It rocks one cycle every three and a half seconds, and makes your diaphragm and other organs move up and down, to compress and release your lungs. As your feet hit the bottom of the tilt, you inhale. As you go backwards, you exhale. I won't leave you. Come on, you've got to try it soon, so let's get going."

As Peg and two orderlies quickly carried me the few feet from the lung to the bed, I was trembling with fear. There was nothing between me and the floor. If they dropped me, I'd break every bone in my helpless body. Suddenly, thank God, I was in contact with a thick mattress with springs under it, much more comfortable than the one on the hard slab in the lung.

"Turn it on, Jack." Peg braced my knees for support. When the fast rocking started, I was sure I would be catapulted off the bed, but to my surprise gravity was my friend. I stayed firm on the bed, and I was breathing, too, a more natural type of breathing, less forceful than the iron lung, though not so deep.

"I did it." No more having to look at Peg in the mirror. I could turn my head enough to see her standing beside me.

"Good for you."

"You didn't give me a choice." I had to speak on the back swing, when the bed was making me exhale.

"But you didn't have to be so brave about it."

"I was scared to death."

She patted my shoulder and went off somewhere with that brisk squeak of rubber soles on the polished wood floor that was unmistakably Peg.

What a triumph. Another way to breathe, another choice. This was progress. My surroundings had changed their focus, giving me a new view from this seesaw. First the world came up toward me, and then it moved away. I was facing the ward now. I could see out of all the windows, until my feet came up and cut off my view. I could see who came and went in the ward. When the door at the end opened, I could see the food cart in the corridor and a visitor out there talking to Peg. I could see iron lungs on the other side and the tops of their inhabitants' heads. I smiled at the man on the opposite rocking bed, but my head went down, and when it came up again, his feet were up, so I didn't know if he saw me.

I rocked for ten minutes that first time, but soon I was able to rock longer and longer each day, and Peg moved me across the room, closer to the nurses' station.

"Doris will be taking care of you from now on. I want to get rid of that disgusting bedsore and start bathing you on the rocking bed. And tell Dottie to bring in some shirts, no more lolling around in those johnnies. Rocking bed patients get dressed every day."

With my bed on the other side of the ward, I was looking at different patients. Opposite me was Alice, who had a waterfall of long, silky blond hair reaching halfway to the floor. She was from Maine, married, with two young children. Was polio worse for men or women? What would happen to her children? Mine needed me, but at least they had their mother part of the time. In some families, both parents had been hit. We were lucky. Dottie was safe, and so were David and Susie. Better me than them. I could never have borne to see any of them go through this hell.

Doris was small, with bright brown eyes and dark curly hair, pretty but all business. Peg was firm, but Doris was a strict top sergeant, a great nurse, but tough.

At seven o'clock the first morning, she greeted me briskly with, "OK, Lou, you're going to rock on your stomach today, so I can treat that hole above your butt."

The orderlies carried me out of the lung and put me on the edge of the bed. Doris stood next to me as a buffer and rapped out the commands.

"One on each side of the bed. Jack takes the shoulders and

Bill the hips. On the count of three, roll him. One, two, three!" Doris threw a pillow under my feet. "Turn on the bed."

My God, I was on my stomach for the first time in four months. My head was swirling. The bed was rocking and the floor kept coming up to meet me. The mattress pressed into my stomach, and I couldn't breathe. Scared as hell, I lost control and crapped all over the place. I could feel it all over my legs and sheets. I smelled like a sewer.

I wept as the orderlies washed me and flipped me back over onto a clean sheet. I was utterly humiliated. Everyone in the ward would know. I couldn't face them.

"Don't open the curtains," I croaked to Doris.

"Not yet, because you're going right back on your stomach. If I let you stop and think about it, you'll fight me every day."

She was right. After that, I turned over every morning to be bathed and to let the air get to the crater at the base of my spine—"the size of a silver dollar," Doris said.

I began to look forward to my daily trips on the rocking bed, and the bed baths became quite a sensuous pleasure. Behind the curtains, Doris gave me a fast, skilled wash and massage, and by the time she got to my genitals, I was aroused.

"Cut that out," she'd say, and throw cold water on me.

Agony! I wanted her, but I didn't. I was half in love with Doris all the time she took care of me, because of the intimacy and dependence, but it was really Dottie I wanted. I longed to be moved away from the nurses' station to a more remote cubicle where my wife could relieve me.

Soon I was rocking the whole day long, like half the others on the ward, and I hated going back to the lung to sleep. The initial dizziness disappeared, although if I stared fixedly at something while I went toward and away from it, the room started to spin around.

41

The beds on the ward were not synchronized, but somewhere along the orbit, you would find yourself rocking together briefly with your neighbor. One of our games to pass the time was to count the number of rocks it took before the beds caught up with each other again, like watching unmatched windshield wipers until they make a sweep in unison.

We practiced talking to each other. My speech didn't fit the breathing rhythm of the bed, so I had to speak very slowly and break the words into segments. We had to strain to be heard over the noise of the motors, and our conversation was disjointed, as we came together at the middle of a swing and then lost each other.

Like prisoners whispering through a ventilator or tapping out a code, we were desperate to talk. Gradually we learned to coordinate our breathing and speech with the bed motion, and our conversations built up the friendships that are the best memories of my time in the rehab center. While the hospital tried to rehabilitate our bodies, we were restoring each other's souls.

On the rocking bed, I've always been able to turn my head sideways, more to the right, since nursing and feeding are always done from that side. If people stand there to show me a catalog illustration or a picture of their grandchildren, they are too close. I've gone by before I can see. Here at home, I have a Plexiglas reading frame over the bed, and books and papers put up there move with me.

Concentrating on reading is the only time I forget I'm rocking, except that the pain is always there. My body is perpetually punished by the movement of its own weight.

What is it like to live on a rocking bed? If you've ever been at sea, you know how it feels to lie in a bunk when the boat is pitching. That's how a rocking bed feels, but more regular than the sea.

Or go back to childhood memories of a garden swing. First the ground recedes on the backswing, then returns to you, and as you kick forward and lean back when your feet go up, the leaves and branches and the sky approach, then rush away again.

The child jumps off the swing. I stay on my bed to stay alive.

five

The Mary MacArthur rehab center was known all over the world for its success in restoring bodies twisted and maimed by the vicious crippler polio. We had physical therapy every day to stretch the muscles of arms, legs, hands, fingers, feet and toes to often agonizing limits.

My therapist was Nancy Warren. She was head of physical therapy, a dog breeder, and a former colonel in the army, strong and supple, with short sandy hair and no makeup.

One day when she was killing me insistently with that extra arm stretch, she asked casually, "Has any movement come back? I'd like to take measurements to see how effective the therapy is."

On the backswing of the bed, she said, "See if you can move your right hand."

Nothing.

"Move your right leg."

Nothing.

"Wiggle your fingers or toes on your right side."

Nothing.

"Try your left hand."

I couldn't believe it. My fingers worked—a little. It hurt terribly, but I could see my fingers move a fraction and my left thumb almost bend. At last I was on my way back.

Wildly excited, I shouted to the whole ward—or what passes

for shouting when you are chronically short of breath. "I knew it! I knew it!" They raised their own cracked version of a cheer.

"Roll your left leg." Nancy was grinning.

It moved very slightly. I couldn't see it, but I could feel it.

"Nice going," she said crisply. "Congratulations."

"I owe a lot to Colonel Warren, an officer and a lady." Nancy saluted and went back to the exercises.

After therapy, the lunch cart appeared, with the volunteers to feed us. I could hardly eat for rejoicing about moving my thumb with the woman who fed me and planning how I was going to start moving bit by bit until it all came back. She was one of our Wellesley surrogate mothers, social ladies who fed us and chatted and joked. They wore nice clothes and smelled like flowers and made us feel we were still sociable human beings.

They hardly ever spilled anything, as the orderlies did, although it's very difficult to feed a man on a rocking bed. He's not like a child in a high chair. You have to synchronize with the bed. Liquids are the worst, because the bed is moving through a forty-five degree arc and you must keep the liquid level, and yet still be moving with the patient's head while he drinks from a straw. The spillers feel like damn fools, while the spillees feel childlike, powerless, and damp.

After lunch, the psychiatrists had an hour with us before the visitors came. Howie Blaine and I had spent some fairly useful hours together by now, and I was less belligerent, although when I told him about my thumb and he asked solemnly, "How do you *feel* about that?" I could have clobbered him. But instead of saying, "How do you think I feel, idiot?" I played the game and waited for Dottie to come flying in, beaming and lively as usual, to hear the tremendous news.

*   *   *

45

The best thing about life in the rehab center was the companionship that developed among the patients. Like survivors in a lifeboat, we grew dependent on each other and very close.

George was only in his early teens, his life not even properly begun. Poor guy, he was having to cope with the volatile moods of adolescence trapped on a rocking bed or caged inside an iron lung with only his ingenuous boy's face and his flaming red hair still out in the world. He had his sulks and silences and his sudden switches to silliness. Then he would tease the nurses and tell us rotten jokes and giggle with the friends who came to see him—the girls gentle and motherly, the boys awkward and embarrassed, knocking large feet against the wheels of the wide rocking beds.

Dick Higgins was not much older, a rich man's dark, handsome son who had got polio at his prep school, where he'd been a popular football hero. He was six foot four and had gone down to about a hundred pounds. He looked like a skeleton on his oversize rocking bed, which was higher off the floor than ours, because it had to swing through a wider arc. I remember that massive frame coming up off the floor like an oil derrick, rocking in the opposite direction from me. And I remember his elegant mother standing on tiptoe on the running board of the bed to feed him the charcoal he had to have every day because of his tricky digestive system.

Except for his stomach, he was better off than most of us, because he had a small amount of movement and could shift his body a little in a wheelchair, controlling his weight with his feet. He could move the muscles of his back enough to help his breathing.

Dick was the gregarious one who could always start a conversation in the ward. If things weren't going too well, he could always make a joke to get us laughing. It wasn't very loud laughter. When you're on a rocking bed, with no abdominal muscles and no spare breath, you can only open your mouth in a wide grin and laugh silently. If I'm with people who breathe by their own lung power and they're killing themselves over a joke, shrieking and gasping and bending double, I'm probably killing myself, too, only they don't know it.

Sneezing isn't any better. You get the nerve irritation, you make all the faces, then from this adult body, comes a Mickey Mouse sneeze—"psst!"—from the nose.

Bert Fern in the next cubicle was a pediatrician and my special friend. Once we could manage to adapt our speech to our beds' rhythms, we had long talks about our past lives and our possible futures, trying to discover the meaning of the random disaster that had hit us. Sometimes we just joked back and forth, because we both had the same sense of humor.

Dottie and I knew the families of all the patients, and they knew ours. She and Bert's wife Mary had become very good friends. Sometimes one of them would go out for sandwiches, and the four of us would share dinner together, although a rocking bed patient shouldn't talk and eat at the same time, and the meal was often disrupted by Bert or me choking and needing emergency help.

In the evening, some of the children were brought into the ward to see the "Mickey Mouse Club," because we had a better television set than they did. Peter came in a wheelchair with a respirator and motor. Before he got worse and died at twelve years old, he had entered a newspaper contest which asked, "What is the most important invention ever made?"

Peter wrote back, "Electricity, because without it I couldn't breathe."

Karen, who could breathe, came on a stretcher pushed by her father, a witty garbage collector who called himself a "Bacteriological Engineer," and small patients came in the little battered wooden pushcarts that were a relic of the old days when Mary MacArthur was a children's convalescent home. Dottie brought in Mouseketeer hats with big ears for everyone, and we all wore them every evening at five o'clock.

The Mickey Mouse Club went through some terrifying experiences, too.

Young George, who could use the difficult technique of "frog breathing," which I hadn't learned yet, was out in a wheelchair at the far end of the hospital. He choked and couldn't breathe, and they were only just able to rush him back to his respirator in time. Helplessly, from our rocking beds, we saw them bring him in, blue and already passed out, each one of us thinking, "It could be me."

Dick's delicate stomach erupted violently in the middle of the night. We all woke and watched in silence and fear as the doctor and nurses hurried in and out of the curtains around his cubicle and finally had to pump out his stomach so that he could get anough air to survive.

"What next?" we thought. "Who next?"

Then it was my turn for terror.

One day I found out what was down that mysterious corridor. There was a room with a huge bathtub set in the floor, and they were going to put me in it.

When I was a kid at summer camp, one of the counselors had gaily pushed me off the end of the dock into twelve feet of water and yelled, "Sink or swim!" I couldn't swim. I flailed, gulped a lot of Maine's coldest lake water, was sure I was drowning, and out of desperation I finally swam. Within a short time, I won a place on the swim team and earned my junior lifesaving certificate, but the scar of that first suffocating terror was there, and I was never again completely at ease in the water.

When I found out that a regular bath in the Hubbard tub was part of the rehab process, those childhood fears resurfaced.

How would I breathe? How would I get out of the water? The thought of being helplessly immersed sharpened the anxiety about suffocation that was always with me.

It had been months since I had been in a tub or shower. A bed bath, even as practiced by Doris, was a poor substitute. I felt grimy and subhuman; so when they said "tub," I was caught between fear and desire. I could refuse the bath and stay subhuman, or risk drowning and come out refreshed, rejuvenated, and a completely clean man for the first time since my illness. In the end, I didn't have a choice. Peg and Doris said I would go in the tub, and that was that.

Saturday was my bath day. On Friday I was very restless and nervous. I lay awake all night worrying about all the things that could go wrong while I was in the water. I remembered a friend who had a mortal fear of flying. She managed to avoid it until finally her husband, a surgeon, was invited to speak in Puerto Rico and wanted her to go with him. For weeks before the trip, she would walk down snow-laden streets, and every time she saw a suntanned face, she'd think, "Look how lucky he is. He's already been South and come back. I still have to go." I could relate to that. I had been envying other patients coming back from their baths, Dick and George and the young mother, with her long hair twisted up on top of her head. God, they were lucky.

Now it was my turn, early in the morning—I would have been too frightened for breakfast anyway. I'd have something to eat afterward, if I made it back to the ward.

To breathe patients at bath time, the staff used a portable device called a TPS that forced air into the lungs through a mask over the nose and mouth controlled by the nurse's thumb rhythmically sliding back and forth over an opening on the outside of the mask. As Peg and two orderlies approached, I felt like a condemned prisoner facing his last mile. They lifted me gently onto a canvas litter on top of a wheeled stretcher, and immediately secured the TPS mask over my face. A few forced breaths, and I was wheeled swiftly to the chamber of water torture.

The short trip seemed to take forever, although I traveled so fast face up under the incandescent lamps that they blurred into a solid streak of light. We whipped around a corner into the hot, humid tub room. The doors closed behind me. I was trapped.

The Hubbard was an oversized stainless steel tub set into the cement floor. Originally designed for water therapy, it was shaped like half an hourglass, wider for the patient's shoulders and head. This Mother Hubbard's cupboard wasn't bare. It was full of what looked like enough water to fill Lake Michigan. It was a big mother.

They gave me a few more breaths from the TPS machine.

"I can't do it," I pleaded.

"Of course, you can."

"I have to use the bedpan."

"Nonsense," they said irritably, but thought better of it. "OK, we'll breathe you while you're on the thing."

How in hell was I supposed to concentrate on shitting and breathing at the same time? Somehow I managed it, although I was flustered and ashamed, never having had a bowel movement with three people standing over me. With all the losses I had suffered—breathing, movement, freedom—the worst blow to my pride was the loss of privacy.

I had no more excuses. The crew attached the canvas litter to a motorized pulley bolted to a steel beam in the ceiling. Gradually I felt the strain of the cords lifting me. I was on my own up there, struggling to breathe. Although I instinctively pulled with my neck muscles as hard and fast as I could, I was frightened and couldn't get enough air. The pulley moved me over the center of the tub, and I hung there like a side of beef on a hook in the slaughterhouse. I felt completely unprotected and out of control. I would fall into the water and drown. I knew it.

Gently and carefully, I was lowered diagonally into the tub with my feet down and the water up to my chest. My heart was pounding. As soon as I was eased into the water, one of the nurses slammed the TPS mask over my face and said, "Breathe with me, Lou. Get into the rhythm and calm down. You're OK."

Concentrating on breathing, I was unaware of the warm water or the people washing me. The bath finished, they removed the mask and lifted me back to the stretcher. The mask was put on again, and after a few breaths I could relax a bit.

Safely back in my rocking bed, swaddled in towels because the rocking motion fanned the air and could cause a chill, I began to breathe comfortably again. I'd done it. I had proved to everyone, and especially to myself, that I could take a bath. Suddenly, I had a great urge to eat—a reward for the victor.

Nancy worked on my muscles like a dedicated demon, but after the first triumph of moving my fingers, there was no more progress. I could still move my left thumb, but that was it.

The little finger of that hand had atrophied and was now crooked. I didn't think much about that, and I hadn't thought that my body had changed much, except for losing weight, so I was shocked when I first saw my legs. Nancy had kept a sheet over them while she worked on me, but in the spring, when the weather got warmer, she pushed up the sheet, and I saw two wasted skeleton legs that looked as if they had barely survived a concentration camp.

The muscles had gone and, with them, the power that had sprung from my legs to run and jump and dance. Where were the legs that won all those dance contests when I was young? Where were the strong arms that had swung a golf club and smashed a tennis ball over the net?

51

I was bitter about my loss and often reduced to tears. The unfairness of it all drove me into some black moods. Dottie comforted and cheered me through the bad times of despair. My father tried to help, but he was still knocked back by my illness and was withdrawing more and more into himself.

My Uncle Hy, who had lived with us when I was a boy, was a greater strength to me. From the time I was three, I had had two fathers, my gentle biological one who was my best friend and strict Uncle Hy who called me "Sam" and taught me about books and music and table manners and self-control and consideration for other people.

When I was in the rehab center, he would go to restaurants and get steak and a baked potato on a special covered dish and bring it in to feed to me. If the nurses thought it was an exotic diet for a polio patient, they probably figured that I was so ill anyway, I might as well have what I liked.

Everybody watched Uncle Hy when he came into the ward, tall and lean and well-dressed, carrying himself like a lord.

"Hi, Sam, how do you feel?"

"Not so good, Uncle Hy."

When I seemed worse, his long face would look stricken. Desperately, he would try to think of something that would cheer me up. He would tell me jokes, of which he had an inexhaustible stock.

No smile from me. "Lou, my boy, I'll tell you what I'll do. I'll go and get your mother and bring her in. Do you both good."

Or, "Tell you what, Sam. I'll go out and get some tenderloin tips and french fries. Do you all the good in the world."

Besides family, there were many faithful friends who visited me at Wellesley and have been around ever since. I had always made friends easily, and perhaps taken some of the good ones too much for granted, but now I found out how much I needed

52

them. Eugene O'Neill declared that most people want to avoid seeing life as it really is, but my good friends looked at my calamity squarely and then at themselves, to see what they could do about it.

Alan, my golf partner, was a small dynamic man, full of voluble jokes and enthusiasms and marvelous ideas that had to be acted on instantly. The patient, sensitive understanding he showed me in the hospital was something I'd never seen in him before. But then, he'd never seen me cry.

We had a new friendship now, much deeper and more binding. When I was depressed and negative, he didn't try to tease me out of it, but he knew when I needed his energy and jokes and when to nudge me out of taking myself too seriously.

Everyone in the ward loved him because he was so entertaining and full of life. When children were discharged, he gave them a puppy, and when one of the men left, he would give him one of the best pairs of shoes from his factory as a promise that he would walk again: "I hope you wear them out fast."

Milt, my old friend from high school, was the opposite of Alan, large and athletic, and very gentle and quiet. I still would rather have Milt pick me up and carry me than anyone else. He's not going to drop me, and he's not going to hurt me, and he puts me down like a feather.

One evening, Milt came in after work—he made shoes too—and found us all in our mouse-ear hats, trying to see the television screen. He didn't say anything, but a few days later he came back with a new set that had a huge screen that everyone in the ward could see.

Milt, Alan, Milt's wife (friendly, comforting Elaine, who spent more time with me than any other woman except Dottie), Bob, and Sonny—these were the special friends who helped me to survive.

After lights out on New Year's Eve, we were still awake

with our radios on. I was feeling sad and wistful about other New Years I had celebrated when suddenly all these friends and some others came bursting into the darkened ward.

"Happy New Year!"

They had come from a party with bottles of champagne and plates of hors d'oeuvres for us. We all celebrated—whatever we had to celebrate. For me, it was my friends.

Although I was rocking all day, I had to go back every night to my iron womb to sleep. The lung was secure, but claustrophobic. After six months of it, I was longing for more freedom.

One day in January I could see during the upswing of the bed that a light snowfall had covered the low hill beyond the window. At the bottom, the branches of the big elms glistened in the late morning sun with millions of white flakes just beginning to melt.

Intent on the view that was my whole outside world, I didn't realize that Doris was standing by my bed. She was holding a pale blue plastic shell, like the chestpiece of a suit of armor.

"What's that?" I asked on the backswing.

"A cuirass, a sort of mini-lung."

"How does it work?"

"See this opening at the top? One end of a hose goes in there, and the other end is attached to a motor. It's like artificial respiration. We strap it over your abdomen and chest while you're rocking, then turn off the bed and connect the hose right away. You won't have to seesaw all day, and after a while you can even sleep in it."

"No more iron lung?"

"Kiss it good-bye. We'll even be able to get you into a wheelchair."

Wheelchair! The last one I'd sat in had been in the emergency room at Mass. General, and I'd hated it. Now my fondest dream was to be able to roll in and out of the ward, get some new views, explore, and perhaps find a secret room where I could be alone with Dottie . . .

An orderly pushed the motor close to my bed, and he and Doris strapped the shell to my chest. It seemed awfully small. How could it breathe me?

"If there's a problem, I'll turn the bed back on at once," Doris had said, but I didn't trust her. When you can't breathe by yourself, you don't trust anybody. She switched off the bed, and it was a breathless eternity before they pushed the hose into the hole in the chest piece. It moved, but only slightly. It wasn't giving me enough air. I panicked and began to click my tongue for help—the paralyzed patient's SOS— my eyes signaling wildly.

Doris quickly turned on the bed and took off the cuirass. "Sorry, Lou," she said calmly, "I forgot how broad your chest was. You're more of a stomach breather, aren't you?"

When she tried a deeper and larger shell, I got so much air I thought my lungs would burst. I did my Mayday clicking till they cut down the pressure. Soon I was breathing easily, five, ten, twenty minutes, and it was still working.

"That's enough for today." Doris disconnected the hose and switched the bed back on.

"What about the wheelchair?" I was impatient to do it all.

"Soon." Doris smiled and patted my face gently, a thing she hardly ever did. "Right now, you need a shave."

My friends in the ward had been watching anxiously. "Good work, Lou!" Dick twisted his long back to get more breath to call across the room.

We all shared our triumphs and our pain. We couldn't shout to each other, but we got news from the nurses and passed messages from bed to bed and through the grapevine of our visitors.

"First step to getting out of here," Bert said, rocking next to me. "I'll go with you."

55

Dottie Lou's eventual homecoming was the hope that kept us both going through all the long months of his sickness. I was with him every day, first at the hospital and then at the rehab center. The nurse and later a series of baby sitters lived with me and the children, sleeping on the sofa in the living room of our small apartment. I would spend some time with David and Susie in the morning and then go off to be with Lou at Mary MacArthur from noon until about eleven o'clock at night, every day for fourteen months.

I didn't question it. When my brother was ill in the hospital, his wife and my mother were with him all the time, so I knew that I must do the same. I didn't think of it as a hardship. I just went off every day as if I were going to work. I didn't pine for the life of the outside world, because I was never in that life anymore. I had forgotten what it was like.

Quick morning trips to the bank, the stores, the park with the children, and then I would hurry to the rehab center, where Lou was watching anxiously for me, ready to have a fit if I didn't turn up on time. I was never late. I never took a day off. Other visitors came and went, and Bert Fern's wife Mary used to miss a day now and then or go away for a weekend. But allowing me to do that wasn't in Lou's repertoire, and I never suggested it.

He needed me so badly. When you can't move or breathe, you need constant attention, but if you're on a ward with seven other people who can't move or breathe either, you have to wait your turn for the nurses. I did almost everything for him. Later, when he could be in a wheelchair, I pushed him around the center, and we would find quiet corners where we could be alone together, away from the public life of the ward.

Mary MacArthur was Lou's whole world, and it became mine, too. The other patients and their families were our circle of friends, and our social life was the news and jokes we exchanged and the food we shared in the evenings when most of the visitors came.

I am a member of an exclusive club. I am one of eight adult quadriplegics confined in a ward of a rehab center, who are all dependent on mechanical respiration to exist. It's a mid-winter Sunday morning, and I'm waiting for a priest to finish Communion with six of my friends. I envy the Catholics the visits from their priest and the comfort they get from the ritual. No rabbi has ever come near me, either here or at Mass. General.

Through a large window across the room, I see snow falling, covering everything with a mantle of grayish white, making the outside view as dead as the inside, where our unmoving bodies lie. While I wait for the priest to go and breakfast to arrive, my mind wanders once more over the eternal questions. I'm confused and mystified by what has happened to me. Where am I going to find the strength to survive this adversity? Not from God, since God has forsaken me. What's the use of punishment if you don't know what sin you have committed to deserve it?

Those who have had Communion have reaffirmed their faith. I hope they feel better, but can you reconcile this human condition around me with religious faith? As a youngster, I skipped Sunday school as often as possible, but one thing remains clear in my memory: the firm Jewish belief that there is a purpose to life on earth because some part of that life is eternal. Since God has given sanctity to the human body, what happens to it in this life will determine its future, not here, but in another place and time.

I believe that, and yet I can't accept what's happened to me. That's why I'm still fighting with the doctors here. I believe my paralysis is only temporary. I use a chest piece and a wheelchair, don't I? That's progress. Look, I can move my left thumb. Eventually the rest of my movement will come back, and I'll walk out of here, as I walked into the emergency room at Massachusetts General centuries ago.

The priest has gone, and I smell bacon. Outside, the snow is drifting and beginning to pile up, but Dottie will get here somehow. She's never missed a day since I've been incarcerated. I need her. Her undimmed enthusiasm for life is infectious. I've never seen her weaken or cry, but I wonder what she's like when she's alone in her room at home. Our room. The psychiatrist warns against this, but I've become completely dependent on Dottie. She's gentler and more competent than the nurses. In spite of these bizarre surroundings, we're very intimate and open with each other, able to share all our feelings. Some marriages have broken up because of this terrible illness. Dottie and I are closer than we've ever been.

Later, as the bed seesaws to the top of the cycle, I catch a glimpse of Dottie talking to the children at the end of the ward. Thank God, she's here. She makes this half-life more bearable. The flakes of snow glisten in her hair and mix in with the white streaks that are beginning to show, even though she's only twenty-five.

She comes smiling up to the bed. "Look what I've got for you!" A lemon meringue pie, my favorite. "Thought this would pep you up on this miserable day."

She gets plates and forks from the kitchen, and we enjoy the pie together. We talk about the children and what's going on at home. I tell her the news of the ward—who was sick in the night, why the night nurse was impatient, what I had for breakfast. When I first came here, we made plans for what we would do when I got out. These days, we don't talk much about the cloudy future.

But I tell her at last, "I keep thinking about tomorrow."

"What happens tomorrow?"

"Grand rounds of the doctors. I'm going to make them talk

about my progress. It's unbearably slow. At this rate, it's going to be months before I walk out of this place."

Dottie keeps a smile on her face, so that I won't guess at the stab of pain that wrenches her.

In a horseshoe pattern, the senior staff stood around my bed. The physician in charge was Dr. Trott, who was the center's orthopedic doctor. My problems were more medical than orthopedic, and I didn't have much confidence in him. He wasn't the kind of doctor you got to know intimately. He breezed through the ward with a permanent smile and would stop to talk to me about big band music, which was about the only thing we had in common. At fifteen, I used to be a drummer, but not with a group. I just drummed away at home in a peaceful fantasy that I was playing with a band.

"Got any new Benny Goodman albums?" Dr. Trott asked me.

We chatted about nothing much for a while, until I asked bluntly, "When am I going to walk out of here?"

In the silence, the respirator motors sounded louder. Why didn't the doctor answer me? He looked embarrassed. He was a fair-skinned man who flushed easily. He waited until the rest of the group drifted off to the next patient before he spoke.

"We, er . . . we don't believe you'll ever walk again, Lou. And I may as well tell you that I don't think you'll ever breathe again without mechanical assistance."

I stared at him. "Say that again."

He did.

I heard myself scream, "You sonofabitch, you're lying!" It can't have been a loud scream, but its resonance in my head was loud. "One of these days, I'm going to walk into your office and smack you right in the teeth!"

"I hope you do," he said quietly, "I hope you do. I'm sorry, Lou."

I didn't want his compassion. I turned my head away, and he moved on.

In this crowded ward, I was completely alone and weeping. What the hell kind of a dirty trick was this? I began to curse, a futile stream of crude abuse, and no one tried to stop me. Dottie, where's Dottie? My glasses were so steamed up, I couldn't see anything. Peg came over, took them off, wiped my eyes, and replaced the glasses without a word. I was left to the turmoil of my thoughts.

The man's crazy. He doesn't know the guy he's talking to. How can he be dumb enough to think I'd give up that easily? He's wrong, he's wrong. Dottie, Dottie, come and tell me he's wrong . . .

If it was true, I was done for. The reason I had survived and hung on and done well here was that I still had hope. I was frantic when Dottie arrived.

"You know what that bastard said?" In a frenzy of terror and tears, I told her. She tried to comfort me, but her face was anguished and her hands were trembling. She called Bill Berenberg, the pediatrician who had helped us from the beginning of this nightmare.

"It's still too early to tell." He tried to reassure her cautiously. "He may get some more muscle function back." This calmed us for the moment. We grasped at this shred of hope.

Dottie When I went out to the visitors' room for a cigarette, the wife of one of the other patients followed to comfort me.

"We've all had news like this," she said. "No one on this ward is ever going to walk again."

I felt sick, but I went back to the ward and started to try to rebuild Lou's optimism, although I didn't feel at all optimistic myself. Ever since Frank Austen had told me "Lou will probably always need mechanical assistance to breathe," it had been at the back of my mind that he might always be paralyzed. I had refused to accept this, but now for the first time I allowed myself to admit that our lives would never be the same again.

six

Although I didn't know it at the time, I had embarked on the quest that has been at the center of my life ever since—to find a meaning and a purpose for my life.

I had always been a physical person and an athlete. Skill and strength at sports had meant everything to me. It was what I did best, and it was my chief source of self-esteem and independence. If that was gone, what did I have to offer the world? I'd be taking from everyone all the time, never giving.

I had been a vital, active man in the prime of life, and now I was trapped in a dead body with only the use of a few neck muscles and a thumb. How could I be a husband to Dottie? What could I do for my young children? I'd been an energetic and successful salesman, developing a good group of customers and making a small name for myself, but how could a man earn a living with one thumb and total respiratory failure?

I was alive. That was about all. I had loved life, fully and passionately. "But I guess it wasn't life itself I loved," I told Dottie now. "It was *my* life, the way it was. What have I got to live for now, if that damn doctor is right?"

"You're asking too much, Lou," she said. "You want the answer in a blinding flash of light." She took my hand. "You'll find it, but not all at once. We'll work for it together."

I lay there in my lifeless body, thinking of the unthinkable future and the lost, exuberant life we had so recently shared. "I've got to have some purpose, some hope . . . "

"You will."

"How?"

"I don't know, but I believe in you, and I love you. I'll give you all the support I can."

"Give me some answers."

She shook her head. "I don't have them. *You* do. Small, everyday ones. I guess you just build on those till you reach what you're looking for."

I was silent for a while. Then I said grimly, "I hate to lose."

"That's more like you."

"I can either just lie here and vegetate and let life go past me, or I can try to control my goddamn rocking world. I never gave up before, so why stop trying now?"

She pressed my hand gently. We both felt exhausted, as if we had come a long way together.

As my head came up and I could see out of the opposite window, I noticed that where the snow had melted, the grass on the lawn was much greener. Spring was about to renew the earth.

Now that I could use a chest respirator, on the bed or in a wheelchair, the staff began to talk about getting me ready to go home.

One of the steps on the road to home was learning to use a chest respirator to sleep overnight with my rocking bed turned off, which would mean that I was finally weaned from the womb of the iron monster. The first night, I didn't trust this plastic shell to keep breathing me if I shut my eyes and fell asleep. I only dozed and kept waking to check the sound of the motor, like an anxious passenger on a plane. Each time the night nurse passed by my bed, I asked her the time, hoping that the night was nearly over.

Finally dawn began to light the ward. It was morning, and

I had made it safely through the night. Ecstasy, your name is Louis. Freedom from the iron lung at last! I wasn't only a patient, I was an independent person, too.

The next step was learning the difficult technique of glossopharyngeal breathing, commonly called "frog breathing," because you gulp like a frog. All the work at the rehab center was hard and often painful and frustrating, but this was the worst. Even with Nancy's steadfast help, it took me months to conquer it.

Before I could learn to frog breathe, they had to close my tracheotomy incision. This was traumatic for me, because it meant that secretions that built up in the trachea could no longer be suctioned out by machine. I would have to clear my own air passages. But other people were frog breathing, and if they could, I could. Although I wasn't an athlete anymore, the fighting spirit that had always made me desperate to win was still with me.

Frog breathing is an insurance against power failure. It makes it easier to take baths and move around in a wheelchair and eventually to go out. It also gives you more air to deal with colds and mucus. I couldn't be discharged until I could frog breathe properly.

The technique was discovered by accident in a respirator center in California. A patient was being wheeled down a corridor when the power failed, and they weren't close to emergency power. Instinctively, he began to gulp air to stay alive, and he survived without even losing color until help came. After the emergency, they analyzed what he'd done and began teaching all the other patients how to do it.

In this voluntary method of breathing, any type of respirator must be stopped. The patient learns to shut off the nose with the soft palate, and the tongue uses a series of piston strokes to gather enough air for one breath and force it into the lungs.

Try it. Forget the soft palate. You can hold your nose if

you're not paralyzed. Let out all your breath. Raise the middle of your tongue to firm it against the roof of your mouth, and draw the tongue back with a clicking sound to force air down your throat. Keep doing it. If you've done it right, you'll have air to breathe out.

At first, I could only frog breathe for a few seconds, but during twelve agonizing weeks I learned to breathe for longer and longer periods without a machine. My record was fourteen hours, but I never got used to the strain and anxiety of frog breathing. It was worse than my old days at football training with a tough, sadistic coach. It took tremendous energy and effort, and even when I was becoming an expert, I was still exhausted at the end of each session.

Bert was learning to frog breathe too, and we made up a game—a "frog challenge." He'd do fifteen seconds, I'd do twenty-five. He'd do it for a minute, I'd try for two. Step by step, we built this up until we could both manage several hours, the pair of us side by side in our stationary beds, gulping away like frogs in a swamp.

One day Bert called out to me, "Hey, Lou, I've thought of a job we could do when we get out of here."

"Like what?" None of us had thought that far ahead.

"In a summer camp, teaching a bunch of frogs how to man breathe."

As winter bloomed into spring and the weather warmed, Peg encouraged me to try a short trip outside the hospital in my chest piece. We went to my parents' house in Alan's station wagon with a collapsible wheeled stretcher and the motor for the respirator, backed up by a battery and rectifier, with oxygen and suction equipment, in case. Peg was with us, Alan drove, and Milt came along to help lift me and to deal with all the wires and plugs involved.

Getting me and the equipment into my old home was a difficult business. Getting me out again and back into the wagon was a nightmare. The stretcher knocked into doorways, wires were plugged in wrong, I was in a panic, Alan was frenzied, and Dottie pale and strained. When they put me into the back of the wagon, the four of them were lifting me at different heights, so that I tilted this way and that like a casket being carried down church steps by ill-matched pall-bearers. My head only just missed the top of the door frame.

The trip wasn't worth it. I was worried all the time about power failure. Dottie was too anxious even to sit down. My parents and Uncle Hy were so nervous that they couldn't enjoy this longed-for visit. My mother made agitated conversation and kept wanting to give me food, her first thought for anyone who came into her house, especially her son. My father hovered in the background, inadequate and guilty because there was nothing he could do. Afterward I felt guilty, too, because I hadn't been able to give them what they needed.

"That was awful," I told Peg the next day. "I don't want to go out again."

"Yes, you do. It's like falling off a horse. You have to get up and get on again. Let's go outdoors next time, among new people. You have to get away from this place where everyone's like you and out into the world where you'll be different. But you've got to learn to live as if you weren't."

My old golf course seemed like a good place to go, because it was near enough to get back to the hospital quickly if we had to. I had just had my thirty-first birthday, and it would be pleasantly nostalgic to celebrate it by going back to the place where I had been the happiest in my past life.

I had loved to be out in the fresh air for hours, with the lush green grass under my feet, the feel of the club in my hands, and the thrill of watching the ball take off low, rise into the crystal blue sky, and land exactly where I wanted it.

Although my hands had no power now, they could still feel the leather grip of the club. My mind could remember the intense concentration needed to project the image of the shot, my arms could feel the swing, and my imaginary shot flew straight as an arrow, taking me to golf nirvana.

It was a beautiful day in May. The turf was thicker and greener and the sky even bluer than I remembered. The breeze on my face felt wonderful. In my mind, I thought I could get right up and smack the ball down the middle of the fairway. It didn't make me sad to be on the course, because I still believed I'd play golf again one day, even if it had to be from a wheelchair.

The foursome coming down the sixth hole, a par three, were colorfully dressed. They were still too far away for me to see who they were. I hated them to see me like this. I wanted them to remember me as I was. If they recognized me, I wanted them to say casually, "Let's make a starting time for next season."

I knew this was impossible, but I wasn't ready to give up struggling and hoping. Hadn't the famous Ben Hogan, who made a great comeback himself, written to me, ". . . please keep on battling, you'll defeat this enemy in your life"?

The foursome approached and went past, and one of them stopped and looked back and gave me an uncertain wave.

"Out in the world where you'll be different," Peg had said, and it was obvious how different I was. I knew some of the players who went by us on their way to the pro shop. One or two waved, but none of them came over to me. "I'm the same Lou Sternburg," I wanted to tell them, but they walked on.

Up to now, I had only been among doctors and nurses and other patients, and my family and friends who visited me in the hospital and treated me the same as before. This was my first contact with people who didn't know what to do. Since then, I've experienced it hundreds of times. Some people are afraid of me, afraid to come to my house or to come up to me when I'm out, because they don't know how to behave.

* * *

When I was at Mass. General, the great Red Sox player Ted Williams had come to see me. I was in the most acute stage of polio, half dead and delirious a lot of the time. I thought I had a dream that Dottie kissed my forehead through her mask and whispered, "Lou, you have a visitor."

Painfully, I half opened my eyes to the mirror to see a man in a mask and gown standing behind me. He was so huge that he blocked the light.

"Hi, fella, how you doing?"

"OK," I mumbled.

Dottie said, "This is Ted Williams."

"You're kidding."

"No sir," he said. "I came to see this guy I've heard so much about, to see if I can help."

I couldn't believe it. One of the greatest hitters of all time was in the polio ward, risking infection in the middle of a devastating epidemic.

"They won't let me stay long," Ted said, "since I'm not family."

"I wish you were, then I could get into the games."

"You can. Keep fighting, Lou. You'll be at a game sooner than you think."

When he left, he said, "See you again," but I didn't believe it. I still thought it was a dream of my delirium.

It was a summer day in June when, true to his promise, Ted Williams returned. When he came through the corridor and spotted me in the rear corner of the rehab ward, he called out in a booming voice, "You look great, you son of a bitch."

That was no dream I had at Mass. General. He arrived alongside the bed, a handsome giant with huge shoulders, who immediately got down on his knees to figure out how the rocking bed worked.

"How about some fishing at the end of the season, Lou?" I was glad his voice was loud. Everyone in the ward could hear.

"After the series?"

"Sure."

"I don't know that I . . . " Oh hell, he wouldn't want to hear my troubles. But I asked him, "Ted, what do you do when you get into a batting slump? I seem to be in one right now."

He laughed. "I check to see if my head is still when I'm swinging, and then I just try to meet the ball. It didn't come easy. I had to work at it every day. Like you do. Here Lou, I brought you this little rubber ball to squeeze. You'll get stronger."

I hadn't a hope of squeezing the ball. I couldn't take it from him, so he put it by the pillow under my right hand.

"Want to come to a game? The Yankees are coming to town two weeks from Wednesday. I'll fix it." He went off, followed by an admiring crowd, and stopped to talk to every patient on his way out.

Dick and I went to the game with Peg, Dottie, Alan and Milt, and a couple of orderlies. When we were unloaded in the players' parking lot, everyone looked at us, and I felt painfully self-conscious. Dick and I were plugged into electric outlets behind the screen at home plate, and Ted spotted our wheelchairs and brought over several of his team and some of the Bronx Bombers, including Mickey Mantle, short and muscular, and Yogi Berra, funny and very friendly.

Dick gloried in it all, but I couldn't get used to being conspicuous. I had been rather shy as a child and teenager, but this defenseless embarrassment was something new, and much worse.

The memory of how I had felt tormented me for a long time. Would I always feel like this?

The chest piece was squeezing the flesh against my rib cage eighteen times a minute. It hurt. Should I call Doris to ease the pain for the last time?

Today after fourteen months, I was cutting the umbilical cord of the mother hospital and finally going home. When I was there, would I wake Dottie to put in a pad to stop the constant pain or would I eventually learn to live with it?

I called Doris and had to wait till she was finished with someone else. At home at least I would be the only one, and I wouldn't have to wait. Or would I? Who was going to come first in our household, me or the children? God, we'd have to make decisions all the time in this new life I was headed for.

But the big decision had been made. Dottie had found a dream house in Newton on the corner of a little-used street, near a fire house and schools, and halfway between the Boston hospitals and this rehab unit. In case of emergencies, my doctor lived only a few blocks away.

The children would be upstairs, and the dining room in the middle of the house had been converted for my rocking bed, with wood-paneled walls, bedding and nursing equipment shut away in cabinets, and shelves for books and records and television. We wanted it to look like a man's favorite room, unclinical, homey, and comfortable for guests. Did we kid ourselves that no one would notice the bed was rocking?

My father had had an emergency generator installed, but my worst anxiety was that we'd lose electric power and the generator wouldn't work, and I'd have to frog breathe to stay alive. What if I panicked and couldn't remember how to do it? I still had nightmares of the gasping terror when they opened the iron lung. What would happen if a hurricane hit us and I couldn't get back to the hospital?

Dottie would know what to do; I'd be safe with her. Every day I hated it when she had to go home and leave me here. Now I'd have her all the time, and I'd have my children, even though I couldn't be much use to them. I would never toss a basketball back and forth with my son or show my daughter what a great dancer I used to be.

Why hadn't the Salk vaccine been ready a few months

earlier? It was available for some children and pregnant women, but there wasn't enough for strong men like me who weren't supposed to get polio. Now there was enough vaccine for everybody, and at least no one else would have to go through this living hell. I was just the poor sucker who got shot on the last day of the war.

Two weeks ago, we had had a trial weekend at home. The kids were excited, friends came in and out, time flew by, and I wasn't alone until nighttime. Here in the ward, we had each other and everyone was in the same boat, but when I had been alone in my room at home, the full catastrophe of being paralyzed had overwhelmed me. Dottie was next door, and I kept calling her to make sure she'd come in. She only stayed long enough to make me comfortable before she gave me a kiss and left me, a steaming cauldron of sexual emotions waiting for release. When I was home for good, we'd have to find some way to make love.

How was Dottie going to manage to be a wife and a nurse and mother as well and not get torn in two between the children and me? They were afraid of me now, the way I was, and I was afraid of them, because there was only one Dottie pie, which I'd had all to myself every day at the hospital, and now they were each going to want a piece.

Even before I got this crazy disease, I thought they took too much of Dottie away from me. I wasn't ready for them, I guess, but now I was so thankful we had them before it was too late. They would help to give me something to live for. Poor young George across the ward, he would probably never marry or have children. What would his reason for living be?

Part of mine would be to support my family. I'd have plenty of time, God knows, and I couldn't just rock and watch television all day. Since the trial weekend, I could see that Dottie would need help, and we couldn't afford it unless I could earn some money for her. If I went back to being a salesman, would my old customers agree to deal with me over the telephone?

I'd educate myself. I'd read all the books I should have read when I was playing football and chasing girls. Before polio, I was all body and no head. Now I was all head and no body. My brain was all I had to make my life productive, and I'd use it to understand and accept what had happened, and go on with my life from there.

Doris interrupted my thoughts with a basin and a wet washcloth.

"This is the last day you'll run my life, Sergeant," I told her.

"Yup." She went to work.

"I'll miss you though."

"No, you won't. Most helpless male patients think they're in love with the nurse." So she'd noticed. "Doesn't mean a thing."

"Will you miss me?"

"Sure, Lou. A nurse can't help loving a patient who's dependent on her. Doesn't mean a thing either."

Before she switched on the rocking bed, she disconnected the hose and removed the painful chest piece.

"Scratch me," I ordered. "I know how women feel when they get out of their girdles."

After my last hospital breakfast of orange juice, overcooked oatmeal, and tea, Doris and an orderly dressed me while I frog breathed. I was ready to go.

I would miss this place though. All my friends here, Bert and Dick and George and Jim and Alice with her beautiful long hair, we had all decided long ago that polio only attacked special people who knew how to laugh. I would miss all the jokes we'd shared, the worse the day, the funnier the jokes. Could I keep my sense of humor alone at home, without this wonderful companionship?

Saying good-bye to all of them was very hard. I was the first of our lot to be discharged. Some of them were leaving soon. Others didn't know. I had once envied Dick, because he had more movement than I did. Now I saw envy in his face as I was wheeled by his bed.

Dottie had brought Mike, a student who had been an orderly here. He was moving in with us, the first of a long and varied line of Sternburg alumni from all over the world. Peg was coming with us on the trip home. She had made up for us a guide to caring for a respiratory quadriplegic at home and had helped Dottie choose the house and plan my new room. She wanted to see me safely installed.

Where was my motorcade? The streets of Wellesley and Newton should be lined with people cheering and waving because I had won my battle to survive. It should be an open limousine for my triumphant return, but it had to be an ambulance. All I could see were the tops of the trees with leaves beginning to be colored by fall. Nobody lined the streets, but when we stopped, I saw neighborhood faces pressed to the ambulance windows, tense with an anxiety that changed to happiness when they saw me smiling.

Indoors, Mike cradled my head and shoulders, Peg put one arm under the small of my back and the other under my thighs, and Dottie held my knees and ankles. Together they lifted me gently from the stretcher and put me into my wheelchair.

Peg straightened up and stood looking down at me. Confident and clever, this tall, gawky blonde had been my true friend.

"Good-bye and good luck," she said. I couldn't see the expression in her eyes behind her thick glasses.

"Thanks for everything, Peg." What could I possibly say that would be enough? "I hope you make it into medical school, but I'm glad you waited till after I left."

She bent to kiss me, hugged Dottie, and went away.

Through the window, I saw the ambulance turn around and

head back to the hospital. For a brief moment, I felt abandoned. Then the phone started to ring, and the friends who had been helping Dottie to get the house ready came crowding in. Dottie wheeled me all over the ground floor. Dear Elaine was putting plates and glasses away in the kitchen. The living room was filled with flowers. In my room, my favorite pictures were on the walls, my books were on the shelves, and the bright fall sun shone warmly through the windows. I was home to stay.

seven

We never thought it would be easy. It was only possible because Dottie, with some help from Mike, devoted herself to taking care of me twenty-four hours a day, as well as running the house and looking after our two small children.

How she managed it, I don't know, and when we look back at it, neither does she. But she had tremendous practical energy, and from somewhere within her she summoned up a superhuman strength and endurance, as people do when they are faced with the impossible.

After the excitement and euphoria of coming home, we settled more soberly into our day-by-day routine, and Dottie learned all the slow and complicated details of nursing a paralyzed polio patient. She fed me and bathed me and dealt with bottles and bedpans, and massaged pressure points and changed my position constantly. She got out of bed ten or twelve times a night because I was thirsty or choking or in pain or afraid or lonely. With a canvas sling under me, she could get me out of bed and into the wheelchair with the hydraulic lifter, but if Mike and anyone else was there, it was easier for the three of them to carry me back to the bed. We didn't make enough use of Mike because, although Doris and the women at the hospital had done everything, I wasn't ready to let a man do intimate things for me. And in any case Dottie insisted on doing ninety-nine percent of the work herself.

One minute she would be feeding the children in the kitchen, then back into my room to move my hand into the right position on the pillow, back to shovel another spoonful into Susie, back through the door to give me a sip of water, back to wipe up what David had spilled and take the clothes out of the washing machine, back to me in a great hurry to push my chest to help me cough. Our children got colds and David's friends brought in colds, and I caught all of them, one of the worst things that can happen to a respiratory paralyzed polio victim. You don't have enough lung power to cough, but if you don't cough, you may choke, or eventually get pneumonia.

In the middle of whatever she was doing for the children, Dottie would have to run in to me, stop the bed, turn me over with my head lower than my feet, and pound on my back to drain the mucus out. It might take ten turns and poundings to accomplish what one cough would do for an ordinary person.

"All right now?" Dottie could hear the children screaming from another part of the house.

"Where are you going?"

"I'll be right back."

I wasn't really aware of how dependent I was on her nor of what a colossal job she was doing. I was too absorbed in my pain and my own struggle to survive. But if I noticed her exhaustion and said, "This is too much for you," she would only laugh and shrug it off.

"Better than having to go to the hospital every day."

For me, it was a whole world of difference from the hospital. At home, I was the center of everyone's attention and could control what I did and when I did it, instead of being one of the inmates controlled by the hospital rules. I was with my children, and Dottie was there all the time, which brought my life a little closer to normal.

On the other hand, I now had to worry about money and how we were going to be able to keep things going. And I missed the activity of the ward and most of all the comradeship. Now when I was in pain, there was no one else in pain to share it with. I missed Bert terribly. I'd sit in my wheelchair and frog breathe, but it wasn't the same without him next to me, competing. Now there was no one but myself to beat. Although Dottie was constantly with me, and visitors came in and out, I spent a lot of time on my own, a very lonely frog breather.

Sometimes my little room in the middle of the house was like Grand Central Station. It was on the way to everywhere for everybody. The children would run through on their way to the kitchen to open the ice box door—"Shut that door!" When family and friends weren't coming in, it was the milkman and the bread man and the man who brought eggs and chickens coming through to check me out, the bread man usually coughing.

The telephone rang all the time. "How is he?" "How's he doing?" "How's Lou?" It was thoughtful of them, but it drove me crazy. Dottie always had to stop what she was doing to answer it, and I would be ten times angrier than the ordinary husband gets when his wife is always talking on the phone.

At first, I would be on the rocking bed until the afternoon, when Dottie would get me up in the wheelchair. Then I'd frog breathe and watch television until she pushed me into the kitchen so we could have supper with David and Susie. That was usually a disaster. The children and I were both tired. I was trying to eat and frog breathe at the same time, which is never a good idea. We drove each other crazy, and Dottie couldn't handle us. We fought as if we were the same age, while she tried to feed me, and jump up after them all the time, get a few bites herself, and try to keep the peace in the tumult of the crowded kitchen.

I competed with the children for her attention. I was selfish and very possessive of her. Before I got sick, Dottie and I had been very involved with each other, but I had always wanted her to be independent. I had seen my mother live in total dependence on my father, either from choice or meekly following her Polish-Jewish traditions. She devoted her life to her husband and children and she never worked or drove a car or even wrote a check. She was a happy, smiling woman, but I felt that she had been only half alive. Even if it was what she wanted, she should have wanted more. Dottie was lively and clever and ambitious. She had graduated from Smith and earned a good salary keeping the accounts in her father's clothing store. I never wanted to tie her down, but now here I was, doing just that.

Gradually I spent more time in bed and less in the chair, and we stopped trying to have family suppers. After the children were in bed, Dottie would light candles in my room, and although I couldn't talk while she fed me, as long as I didn't choke, we'd have a semblance of a cozy dinner together.

When David and Susie were not taking Dottie away from me, I loved having them around. Now that I had nothing else to do but rock all day, I wished I could help with the baby and regretted having been so squeamish about changing diapers when David was little. Now, with Susie it was too late.

The children enjoyed having me at home, even though I couldn't play with them. Most parents are always on the move, and I think they liked having me consistently in one place, available for chatter at any time. Their favorite game was to ride on the end of the rocking bed, perched between my feet, as it swung up and down. I can see Susie now, hanging onto my lifeless feet, mouth open as the bed went up toward the ceiling, staring at me with huge dark eyes. It was almost as good as holding her.

Besides everything she had to do for me, Dottie had to cope with all the visitors. She was always answering the doorbell, and she couldn't just let them come in and see me and then find their way out. She had to give them coffee and bake

cookies for them and pretend she had time to chat with them
and see them to the door and ask them about their own lives.
And all the time she had to keep an ear out for me and the
children.

Our families and all our good friends came often. One or
two of the neighbors came quite soon after I got home, with
flowers or cake, and stayed in the hall at first and only talked
to Dottie. On the next visit, they might venture to my room
and wave from the doorway. Next time, they'd come right
in.

Most people were startled by the size and movement of
the bed. I would see them hesitate as they came in, wanting
to take in the whole scene for a moment and understand it
before they came closer. A few walked right up to me, but
most of them came toward me in a wide, cautious circle. I'd
have to put them at their ease to reassure them that this wasn't
a horror show. They'd be solemn and careful at first, until
they realized that it was all right to relax and laugh. It was
still the same old Lou, who just happened to be rocking. Many
people never came. They were afraid of me, I think, and
afraid of their own inadequacy. They stayed away because
they couldn't help me and because they didn't know what to
say. It's still like that. Some of the people we'd like to see
have never come. Some who do come can hardly talk, because
they're afraid of saying the wrong thing. I can see fear in their
faces. They're worried, tense, and pale. They stutter a bit
and grope for words, so I have to carry the conversation. If
they won't relax, I start talking about them—what they do,
what they like. It's my old salesman's technique, except that
now I have to sell myself.

Since I can't shake hands, they don't know how to greet
me. If a man sticks out his hand, it's left there in the air. He
has to take it back, and I have to make a joke of it for him,
to save embarrassment. To avoid this, I cover my hands when

I'm out in winter. When it's warm, there are always some people who insist on squeezing my hand. They damn near kill me, but not one has broken a finger yet.

Some women want to kiss me hello or good-bye, which is all right, as long as they don't give me a cold. I make them feel maternal, as if I were in my second helpless childhood, and I'm no threat to them, since I can't respond. But it's hard to kiss a man in a rocking bed whose face is either dropping back away from you or bumping up toward you and then gone by. Dottie can do it. The others just have to lay their faces near mine and let their heads travel with me.

The family and close friends had all been with me in the hospital, so they were used to the bed, and me. My father could even shave me with a straight razor while I rocked. Uncle Hy was still bringing in food.

He would call up. "How'd you like some fresh corn?" He'd arrive and make Dottie stop whatever five or six things she was doing and boil the corn. Then he'd hold the ear for me while I bit off the kernels, wiping the butter from my chin, very neat and precise, making sure I went along the whole ear and didn't leave anything on it. Then he'd go away and wash his long fingers and come back and put on some music and listen to it with me, sitting tidily, very upright, with his clothes pressed, keeping up his standards in this strange, chaotic household.

When my good friend Milt came, he sprawled in his chair, not saying much, but shifting his large body from time to time.

"I wish I could do that, Milt," I'd say, tormented by aches and itches and twitching nerves, and he'd jump up and spend a long time patiently trying new positions for my arms and my fingers, scratching me where I itched, raising or lowering the head or foot of the bed, propping me a little sideways with foam padding under one hip.

Then he'd go back and sit down and think and watch me,

and Dottie would come in on the wind of her own speed and energy and rearrange me all over again.

Al and Evelyn Clark lived across the street. He came in every day after work, and sometimes Dottie would go to their house for a break while Al stayed with me. I usually greeted him with, "Hi, Uncle Al, how's business?" But if I'd had a bad day with a lot of pain, it would be only, "Hi, Al." So he'd sit on a high stool by the bed and tell me what was going on out there in the world of business and make jokes about characters we knew and clown and make me laugh; he'd entertain me with amazing stories of his days as an ace pilot in the Marine Corps.

He'd get up and prowl about the room when he got sleepy, because the movement of the bed is hypnotic. Frank Austen, my doctor friend from Mass. General who was still dealing with iron lungs, used to turn off the bed and make me frog breathe when he came. He was always so overworked and tired that the bed would put him to sleep in fifteen minutes.

Peg came from the rehab and remained our friend for many years after she went on to medical school. Doris never came, which was not surprising and all right with me. Although I had been infatuated with that tough, capable young woman who had held my life in her hands, I didn't miss her after I came home. She was part of that other world, which now had no claim on me.

It was difficult to find a new doctor to take care of me after I got home. Poliomyelitis was still thought of as a children's disease, and most doctors with an adult practice knew very little about it. So our children's pediatrician, Dr. Berenberg, became my doctor too and stayed with me for two years before he felt I would be better treated by a doctor of adult medicine and referred me to the experienced Dr. Harold Karlin, who has been my doctor ever since and has become a close friend.

I hated losing Bill Berenberg. He was my idea of God. I

trusted him completely, and he would go out of his way to do things for me, which made me feel I really mattered to him. He was a sensitive man, who understood the emotional trauma I was going through as well as the physical damage, but that didn't stop him from giving it to me straight when I needed it. Once when things were very bad because I was competing so outrageously with the children for Dottie's love and attention, he stood by the bed with his hands in his pockets and said, "You're trying to get Dottie to put you first, but you know, Lou, given the choice, any woman would choose her kids before her husband."

That was the sort of talk I couldn't stand. I was insecure enough already, and terrified of abandonment.

"It isn't fair." I took refuge in whining. "The kids can do a lot for themselves, but I can't do anything. I need her more."

"Actually," he said, leaning to the left to keep his eyes on my face while I swung down away from him, "Dottie gives you a hell of a lot more than any other woman I could possibly imagine."

Al said something like that once. He said, "I hope you realize that all the guys are jealous of the kind of a wife you have."

"I know." I had already set foot on the endless guilt trip along which I still slog, trying to find a way to get off. "I'm a possessive, demanding bastard, and she's too good for me."

"She loves you, Lou."

"Yeah, thank God. I hang on to that. She does it all for love."

Dottie I did it because there was nothing else I could do. When Lou first came home, I didn't expect him to be there very long, because I didn't see how anyone could be so ill and not die.

"Take good care of him," Peg said as she shut the door.

"I sure will."

My churning stomach was asking, "How? What if he chokes? I don't have a suction machine. What happens when he sleeps? Do I have to watch him all night? I've never emptied a bedpan in my life. What if no one is here when he needs one? I haven't even had the responsibility of day-to-day care of my own children, let alone a helpless, dependent adult who needs me to keep him going."

The door shut behind our guardian angel. Nothing to do now but plunge in.

"Daddy, can I kiss you?" Three-year-old David breaks the ice for everyone. "I glad you're home. Guess what? Across the street is the Cwarks, and next door is the cat house, and next to that . . . Why are you laughing?"

What fun to be a family again. We're talking together. The phone's ringing, people are walking in and out of the house bringing good wishes, food, cheer. This won't be too hard. We can handle it.

Then Susie wakes up crying from her nap. I've chosen a two-story house, so the children can have their rooms away from the hustle of activity. But now Lou is downstairs in his wheelchair, and Susie needs her diapers changed upstairs. What if Lou can't call when he needs me? Mike will have to stay with Lou while I'm upstairs. This is just the beginning.

The first big problem was getting ourselves into a routine. There were still only so many waking hours in the day and three people who were dependent on me for everything from breathing, scratching, and bathing to keeping the house clean and tidy, seeing that everyone had clean clothes and sheets, preparing the food and feeding it. Susie, at fifteen months, was more independent than Lou, but she needed bathing, dressing, and feeding, and so did he. When and how to do it all and where to cut corners? When would

I bathe and dress and eat? David was only three, and for the last fourteen months our children had hardly seen us. They were longing for love and attention.

Without thinking much about it, I plunged in and did first things first. Whoever seemed to need me the most got the attention. The house came last.

Although I hadn't thought much about how I was going to handle all the everyday complications, I had spent a lot of time thinking about the way I wanted our family to be seen by other people—our friends, the neighbors, the world we lived in. I didn't want any of us to be ashamed of the way we lived or isolated by fear of what other people thought. I wanted our home to be approachable by everyone, not just pointed out as the house where the man on the rocking bed lived. I wanted the children to love Lou as a normal father, even though he wasn't, and to go to him not out of duty but out of desire. I knew that Lou and I would never live a normal life again, but I didn't want that to mean they couldn't live like other children. I never wanted to lose sight of the fact that I had chosen to do this, and they must not be the victims of my choice. Both Lou and I had had wonderful carefree childhoods, and I yearned for that for our children. How would I make it happen?

I was terribly aware of the fragility of life. My brother had died at thirty, and now my husband was struck down. What if something happened to me? If Lou died, I would have to go to work. The most important lesson I wanted to teach my children was independence. That became the cornerstone of their upbringing.

I had always been able to achieve what I wanted. My aim in life in those days was to be the best possible wife, mother, daughter, daughter-in-law, and now nurse. It never occurred to me that this might be impossible. I just went about my business.

Everyone was thrilled to have Lou home, and everyone

wanted to show their support for us, so I left the doors to the house unlocked, and hordes of visitors, delivery men, and the children's friends came and went all the time. And through it all, I had to be the perfect hostess, talking to everyone, always serving food and drinks, never using paper plates or cups, exhausted at the end of the day, with a pile of dirty dishes and a husband to put to bed in a chest respirator.

The phone rang all the time. In those days, I wasn't smart enough to have the laundry on the main floor, so I was always running down to the basement to put mounds of dirty clothes into the washing machine, then back to switch them from the washer to the dryer, and again to retrieve them from the dryer for folding. Of course, every time I went to the basement, the phone rang, so I would have to run upstairs to answer it (my curiosity and Lou's irritation with the noise would never let it go on ringing), and assure the caller that everything was "fine." Then if Lou or David or Susie didn't have a problem that occurred to them when they caught sight of me, I would race back down to finish my task.

Then there was the night. Lou had a micro switch on a gooseneck that he could push with his head, and there were buzzers throughout the house. He would use the buzzer to call whenever no one was around, or if he was choking and couldn't speak.

In the hospital, he had been in an open ward, with the nurses quietly checking on the patients and caring for them. Even if they were with someone behind the blue curtains, one of them would always reappear within a short time, even if it was just to fetch something. So whenever Lou woke, there was always movement and signs of life around him. Now, after I put him in his pajamas (no small feat), fastened the chest cuirass around him, padded all the sore spots, checked the negative pressure on the breathing motor, tucked in the blankets and kissed him good-night, I turned out the lights and left him alone and went to my room, a converted den, about six feet away.

When Lou woke, unable to turn or toss or scratch or move, he was alone in the dark, his helpless body rising and falling inside the life-giving chest shell. His first impulse was to hit the buzzer because he needed reassurance that all was well and that he was safe. This was understandable, but not too good for sleeping. I belted out of my bed (My God, is he *dying?*), and when I reached his bedside, he would only want a sip of water or a leg moved left or right or a pillow punched up under his hand. I dropped back into bed and immediately was sound asleep. The doorbell rang. I must get up to answer it. It rang again, and I realized it was the buzzer. Now what? He forgot to get his nose scratched.

This routine went on nightly anywhere from five to twenty times a night. I was blessed with the ability of youth to conk out as soon as my head hit the pillow. No wonder. I was exhausted. And when I got up in the morning, the whole hectic day was beginning again.

David was a bundle of energy. He never stopped moving from morning till night, and he was constantly in and out of the house. I would try to get him dressed early, so he could be off and running. He always wanted to help me, which takes some patience with a three-year-old, especially when you're a perfectionist. Susie was much more passive, and now that I think back, the poor little thing always seemed to be behind bars. I never had the time to watch her, so she was either in the baby tender, the play pen (with bars), the crib (with bars), or strapped in the stroller. Maybe that's why she fought so hard later on for her independence.

Lou was used to the morning routine at the center. This meant taking off the chest piece, washing his face, giving him a urinal, brushing his teeth, starting the bed rocking, making and feeding him breakfast, putting him on a bedpan, giving him a bed bath, turning him over for a back rub, dressing him in clothes so that he could feel human, and leaving him to rock for the day. In my untrained hands, this little routine took about three hours. Then it was time for lunch. My God, I hadn't even done the breakfast dishes yet.

Meanwhile, the attendant had gone off to his morning classes at nearby Babson College and wouldn't be back until two. Susie was in the baby tender in the kitchen next to Lou's room. I would shovel a mouthful of food into her, run into the next room to do something for Lou, run back for Susie's next spoonful, cut David's sandwich for him . . . Quick! Lou's choking—some water. "I'll be right back, Susie. David, can you answer that phone?"

It was a challenge, and I always liked a challenge. What I find so incredible now is that I also did all the things that other mothers did. I looked for the best nursery schools, made sure my children were clean and dressed in attractive clothes, and tried to give them all the love that was so important in their early years. It never occurred to me that I was being a superwoman. I just did it.

And I didn't think it would be forever.

eight

I was terribly upset when I found out years later that Dottie had been thinking like that. I didn't believe it would be forever either—but for a completely different reason. I still believed that I would walk again.

I hadn't fully realized the truth of my paralysis. I could discuss it intellectually, but I had not accepted it. In my mind now, I sometimes think it's a dream from which I'll wake and find it isn't true.

As late as this morning when I was in the bath tub, I found myself thinking, "What would happen if I got up and walked?" I can feel something there. I can feel my legs walking. I know what turf feels like under my feet. Nothing can rob me of that.

After I came home, I always thought that there would be an end to this. I'd get my movement back. A new therapy would be discovered, a new cure. *I didn't believe that it would always be like this.* That's what kept me going and made me able to live with pain.

The pain was more bearable at first, because I was convinced it would stop one day and be done with and forgotten, like the pain you suffer at the dentist. As time goes on, it has become harder and harder to imagine that.

They can't cut a nerve to relieve me of pain, because if I were paralyzed with no feeling, I would be incontinent and I wouldn't know when something was wrong, like a bedsore developing. I can't take strong painkillers, because they would depress my breathing. I wouldn't anyway, because I don't want to give in and I might get addicted and lose control. That would be the end.

I discovered quite soon, in the converted dining room, that my pain is a two-edged sword. It is both debilitating and motivating. Some days all my energy goes into coping with it. At the same time, it forces me to do something to get rid of it. When I want to be alone, I have to struggle between keeping my solitude and calling someone to move me. We try every possible change of position. The pain is at war with me, and I fight back. So I am still in control. I haven't been conquered. "I thank whatever gods may be,/for my unconquerable soul."

Since I was a boy, enthralled with the noble deeds of bygone heroes, I have thrilled to the promise of W. E. Henley's poem. "I am the master of my fate,/I am the captain of my soul." Even the relentless suffering of thirty years cannot take that away from me.

The pain comes partly from my bones, because the muscles over them have deteriorated and they lie close under the skin, like the front of a shin bone. It's partly from distension and gas created by frog breathing and swallowing air even when I sip through a straw. I have enough gas in me to float on the ceiling and stay there like a helium balloon. Most of my pain, however, comes from having to use the rocking bed.

The air fans me all the time as I travel through it, and the seesaw motion gives my motionless body a sense of mobility, but sometimes it feels like a bed of nails, which pierce my body in pain.

Unlike the Indian fakirs, I have never managed the mastery of mind over matter. Each rock has its own pain. My rear end rests on the fulcrum, and as the foot end drops, the pressure hits my pelvic bone like a driven spike. Cranking the ends up or down and padding me with foam gives some relief, but only for a few hours. Then it starts up somewhere else. I shuttle the pain around, trading it off from one spot to another, but my old enemy never gives up. It never goes away.

The hospital had been a safe place for me, but at home I began to develop fears and anxieties, most of them related to a profound fear of death.

Losing electric power is one of my nightmares. There'll be a local blackout. My generator won't work, and the batteries in the respirator will be dead. I'm always watching for trouble. If the lights flicker because an appliance cuts in, I immediately think, "Are we losing it?"

Al tells me, "If the power fails and the generator fails, I can still pick you up and get you the hell out of here," but I'd have to frog breathe until they could get me to a hospital, and I might be too panicky to do it.

I'm afraid of choking and suffocating and terrified of fires. How would they ever get me out of here if this brown wooden house went up? I go over and over the scene in my mind. Everyone else gets out, and they can't get through the flames to my room . . . a terrible way to die.

We had an attendant named Sam for a while, and when he came back to visit us, he brought a box of fried clams for a treat and put them into the hot oven still in the cardboard carton. When flames came shooting out of the oven, Dottie called the fire department, and they came at once, without sirens and on tiptoe, because I was having a nap, thank God, and the smoke didn't wake me.

Usually, I am very sensitive to any strange smell. Because I am so vulnerable, all my senses have become more aware. If someone only flicks my face, it hurts. Even a gentle touch on the arm or hand can be painful. I used to have a strong handshake, learned as a child from my parents—"Shake hands like a man"—but now, even if I could take someone's hand, the slightest pressure would be agony.

I'm always on the alert for different noises. I lie awake at night with my antennae out, listening, checking out the atmosphere of the house to be sure that all's well. Noises are amplified. Voices shout. A motor bike is deafening. A book dropped on the floor of my room makes me jump.

When the children were small, we had a dachshund called Charlie, who would bark at anything. If a plane went over, he would run through the house barking, while I cringed. Once he ran out of the door and bit the mailman on the leg, and we were sued for a lot of money. We couldn't get rid of Charlie, because the children loved him, but Dottie and I secretly hoped he would disappear. To pay us back, he did it in his own dramatic, disruptive way. He went behind Dottie's car, and she ran over him, poor little guy. Dottie was sobbing and David and Susie were yelling at her, "Murderer! Murderer!"

We had to get another dachshund, but since David and Susie grew up, we haven't had a pet, or let anyone bring one into the house. Another one of my fears is of a cat or dog jumping onto the bed. Flies and biting bugs are bad enough, when you can't brush them off or scratch the itch they leave behind. Once an earwig dropped down on me from a ceiling beam. I dreamed it crawled across my cheek and into my ear, before I woke and realized it wasn't a dream.

Inwardly, my sensitivities became more fragile. I cried a lot in those early days. I was trapped, I thought no one cared, and there was no escape from my plight. If I wept in the daytime, someone would wipe my face, but alone at night the stinging tears would gather in my eyes. Next time you cry in bed, lie on your back without moving your head, and you'll see how painful it is when the tears can't fall or be wiped away.

I still cry now sometimes, for the same reasons, and there is an empty sinking feeling in the pit of my stomach if I let myself contemplate that this is going to go on for the rest of my life.

After all these years I'm better at fantasizing, something most people lose as they grow away from childhood, and I daydream about what I would do if I got out of here and where I would go. I've learned how to control my thoughts. It doesn't always work, but usually I can lead my mind away from despair to anything I want that's more productive.

At first, I could only do that for a short time, but as I began to develop some interests and hobbies, it grew easier to steer my mind away from the physical and emotional pain. One of the attendants got me interested in progressive jazz. He sorted my record and tape collection for me, and we would make tapes of music we heard on the radio. I read a lot, with someone to turn the pages of the book or magazine on the Plexiglas reading rack that moves with the bed. In the evenings, Dottie and I worked on a stamp collection and a coin collection, with which David learned to count, and the attendants built model railway systems for me in my room.

A tank of tropical fish on the counter under the cabinets provided beauty and endless fascination and brought me the friendship of a wonderful man called Hank. He was introduced to me as an expert on fish and has been a true friend and confidant for years.

Hank is tall and dark and spectacularly handsome. He is the president of the highly successful Charles River Laboratories in Boston and also a sweet, genuine man with a lot of common sense and kindness. He was one of the people who helped me get back into my old business as a salesman.

Getting back to work was the thing that helped me the most. It was vitally important to get myself involved again. We needed the money. Our families were generous, but I wasn't going to live off them. I had to help support my wife and children, if I was going to get back any of the self-esteem that had been knocked out of me by this demonic illness.

I couldn't keep records or do any bookkeeping or correspondence, so we made it Dottie's business. She became president of Dot Sales, and I worked for her without salary. Our business was the one I knew, selling the woven labels that go inside clothes. Most people hardly notice these, except when they look to see if it says "Dry clean only" after they've already washed the garment, but the manufacturer and the label maker and maybe an advertising agency as well put a lot of thought and work into the design and logo and color and size. A pattern called a jacquard is made on the same principle as a player piano roll, with cut-out holes, and the labels are woven onto strips. Then another machine cuts and folds or fuses the raw edges.

My friend Lenny Bell from Maine, whose woven labels I'd been selling before I got sick, had already told me in the rehab center that, in exchange for part of the profit, he would turn over to me the output of a loom with a capacity of fifty thousand labels a day. In case he couldn't produce enough to keep me busy, I found an additional supplier, and later others came to me. When you're a sales representative, sources are sometimes easier to get than customers.

Dottie's father was in the garment business, and so were many of his friends and ours. I knew they would help me, and I began to make calls to people who had done business with me before, to see if I could get orders. Dottie would lay the phone against my shoulder or prop it in a holster. She had to stop the rocking bed so the phone wouldn't slip away from my ear, and I frog breathed while I talked.

I started by calling my oldest customers to let them know I was back in circulation again and, even if I couldn't visit them in person, I would do anything they wanted, with my voice.

These people all knew what had happened to me, and most of them took the time to talk with me and gave me at least one order. I thought that was the least they could do, and if they turned me down, it seemed like a slap in the face that I couldn't understand.

I had been tested in a fiery crucible. The world out there owed me something. I wanted special consideration, and yet at the same time I wanted to be treated like a regular salesman. Did I or didn't I want to be treated as normal? I don't think I really knew.

Some customers, like George Sibley, Donald Cohen, and Joel Gordon, would always talk to me however busy they were. "How's it going, Lou? How can I help?" The ones with whom I never connected either didn't care how I was or were too scared of me to answer the phone. They were always "in a meeting" or "busy right now" and hardly ever called me back.

On the phone I was at the disadvantage of being too easy to turn off. I couldn't make an appointment to sit down and talk with them, as I used to do. I only had that short time on the phone to make my pitch, sell my product, and make them like me, so I could set myself up for a reorder. These were busy people who needed to get the most information in the shortest possible time.

If Dottie answered the phone when someone's secretary or buyer called me, she might hear something like, "Mr. Sternburg is nice to do business with. He comes across on the phone as very efficient and fair, and he's honest."

"Thank you," Dottie would say in a crisp, secretarial voice. "I think so, too."

It would take Dottie about two hours to get me ready for the day. Sometimes the current attendant would help. Sometimes he would stay in the kitchen eating breakfast and reading the paper, because I didn't want anyone but Dottie to take care of me, and she didn't think anyone else could do it as well as she could. Which was, and still is, true.

By 11:00 A.M., I was ready to make my first business call. When Dottie picked up the receiver to put it on my shoulder, it connected me with a long-distance operator in Boston.

"How are you today, Mr. Sternburg?"

Because I can't dial, I have come to know dozens of operators over the years. They send me cards, pictures of their families, news of their daughter's graduation. They call us during hurricanes and power failures to check up on me. Some of them have come to see me, and one of them fell in love with me.

I worked for about two hours. After each call, I dictated notes to Dottie or the attendant. Dot Sales began to take off. We were successful in our small way. Before I got sick, I had been involved with one of the best label houses in New England. That company was very loyal to me. While I was a phone salesman, the company grew and I prospered with it. Its success was largely responsible for the addition to our house that took me out of the cramped and populous dining room and into a room of my own.

Picking up my business again was the best way to disassociate myself from the constant pain. The phone calls took my mind away from introspection and self-pity and made me feel useful and productive, so that I began to recover some of my shattered self-esteem.

Sex was the other thing that could get rid of pain for me. Although we didn't have much privacy in my room in the middle of the house, Dottie and I managed to find again the satisfying sex life that had been one of my main reasons for wanting so desperately to get home. My passion was easily aroused. Dottie could still turn me on as she had before, by her laugh, the way she moved, a pair of tight pink slacks . . . Making love was for me a reaffirmation of manhood, of life itself. It was a way to get so involved with something else that I could forget what had happened to me for a while. And it was the best way, as always, for Dottie and me to express our love for each other.

*   *   *

I started to make some short journeys away from the house quite soon after I came home. We bought a secondhand black and red Volkswagen minibus and took the seats out so that my wheelchair could be pushed up a ramp and bolted to the floor.

It was very rough and cumbersome for Dottie to drive, and it didn't give me a comfortable ride, but it got me out of the house and got me moving and made me feel more normal. "Normal" was the word I used to myself for what I wanted to be. I didn't use the chest respirator in the bus. I had it with me, but I frog breathed all the time I was out, so as to be as normal as possible.

When I first started the trips, I was like a space walker out on a tether, away from my center of security. We always had to be able to get home easily, in case. I'd been to the golf course and the Ted Williams baseball game in the rehab center's station wagon, so I wasn't afraid to go out; but after a few trips, alone in the back of the bus, I began to worry about an accident and what would happen if the bolt didn't hold and my chair started to slide. There began to be a constant undercurrent of apprehension. What can go wrong? What's going to happen?

When Dottie took me to Children's Hospital for regular checkups to see if I was getting any movement back, I was all right leaving home and all right when I got to the orthopedic department of the hospital, because they could take care of me there. But the time between takeoff and landing—that was the crunch.

"Anything might happen," I said to Dottie. "We could get ourselves into a hell of a mess that would really screw me up. I'm taking the chance that the other shoe might drop."

She laughed, that energetic, amused laugh of hers that lights up her whole face and everything within range.

"Lou," she said, "don't you realize that the other shoe has already dropped?"

So we took our chances together. Sometimes Mike or Sam or another attendant came with us. Sometimes I went with Dottie alone. She needed help to push me up into the bus, but she could do everything else herself. She had become an expert at getting me off the bed and into the wheelchair, winching me smoothly up in the canvas sling with the hydraulic lifter, and pushing it into the exact position to drop me neatly into my padded chair seat at just the right angle.

She could get me down the bus ramp and winch me back into bed if there was no one at home to help her to carry me. Once she let down the back of the chair to get me at the right angle for lifting, and when she turned away to pull the lifter close, my weight tipped the chair backwards and I ended up with my head on the floor and my feet in yellow socks up in the air, like a beetle helpless on its back.

I yelled. Dottie laughed, and then she began to yell, too, for help. David wandered in from the front yard and ran straight out again, calling to his sister.

"Hey, Susie, come and look at Dad!"

Susie watched with interest while David tried to help Dottie, who was struggling to lift the back of the chair. There was no one else around. Al's wife across the street had dropped the children off when we got home and gone out. I had stopped yelling and started begging, "Get me out of here!" Then I stopped even groaning, because frog breathing was getting very difficult, and I was running short of air.

I was never so glad to see the bread man, with his chronic cough. He brought in a neighbor who was walking past the house, and they got me upright and carried me exhausted to the bed, and Dottie switched on the motor. Show over. The children ran outside again.

Dottie and I went to friends' houses about once a week. With Sam we went to the U. S. Amateur Golf Championship at the Brookline Country Club and watched a brilliant teenager, Jack Nicklaus. We had parked ourselves at a safe distance, and I almost got myself decapitated when he hit an incredible three-hundred-yard drive that whizzed past me.

On our fifth anniversary, instead of the trip to Bermuda we had always promised ourselves, I celebrated by wearing Bermuda shorts. I got a kick out of that, until I looked at what was left of my legs. Then it wasn't funny anymore.

Sometimes friends would invite us to parties, and I always wanted to go, to prove that I hadn't dropped out of the picture and could be like everybody else, but often I ended up wishing I hadn't gone.

People crowded around me when I arrived. Sometimes they treated me as special, and sometimes they took great pains to treat me as if I were the same as I had always been. If they treated me as normal and wandered off to mingle and left me to fend for myself, I was hurt and resentful. If they made a great fuss over me with lavish attention and admiration, I was embarrassed. Parties became situations in which I couldn't win, but I kept on going to them because I had this stubborn macho desire to prove myself, since I felt so insecure.

When I first came home, everyone had said, "It's so wonderful that Lou's alive!" So now I was going out. Wow, even more wonderful! Wonderful to the second power. It may have been wonderful for them, but it really wasn't for me.

"I hope Lou's coming," they said. "That will make the party."

They still say that. "Lou came to my wedding!" That makes them feel good. I'm afraid I've become a bit of a showpiece. Some people have their token blacks. I am your token quadriplegic.

Usually I wouldn't go anywhere without Dottie, but once I went out alone with Sam, who was a student at Boston University, a tall, burly basketball player.

I asked him to take me back to the Mary MacArthur rehab

center, because I wanted to see how the patients I had left behind were doing. Ten of my friends were still there, and although we were all glad to see each other, it didn't quite work out the way I'd planned. I had looked forward to making a triumphant visit from the real world to show them what I could do and how I could live outside the hospital, but they were too turned in on themselves and what they did within the hospital to care much about me.

I don't blame them. I'd have been the same. When the ward was my whole world, I wasn't too interested in what was going on outside, except for hearing news about my children. When people came to see me, I wanted to talk about myself more than about them.

It's different now, because although I am still a prisoner on my rocking bed in my room, my mind has gone out into the world. I know that I need what people from outside can bring to me more than I need what I can give them from myself, which paradoxically may be why they sometimes say that they get a lot from being with me.

I had expected to fit right back in with my old gang at Mary MacArthur. The sense of belonging to a group had been one of the best things there, and I hoped I would recapture that in their welcome. But I couldn't. No one ever can. Instead of closing ranks around me to include me again, my ward mates had closed ranks to fill the gap I'd left, and there was no room for me. I was an outsider.

The only other time I went out without Dottie was to go to Mass. General with Alan and Milt to try to help another polio patient who needed to learn how to frog breathe.

I was wheeled through the same lobby into which I had walked more than two years before. The same light brown walls, same black and white floor, same endless preoccupied traffic of doctors and nurses and technicians and cleaners and visitors and patients. It was very strange. I tried to remember the feverish young man who had walked shakily in here, deathly sick, but still independent. He was twice the weight of the motionless man I was now.

We went up in the same elevator in which I had gone down to the basement in my iron lung. The ward was the same one I had been in before, but there was less light. It seemed to be full of shadows. Alan pushed me over to the corner, where a young woman named Phyllis was in bed, wearing a chest respirator.

I was wearing one too, and I asked Sam to disconnect the air hose. I wanted to show her that, even though I also had respiratory paralysis, frog breathing could give me enough air. I wanted her to see it would be a good thing for her to learn, so she could get out of bed.

She didn't say much. She seemed shy and rather scared. Several of the staff had come in to help and to learn the technique, and they got more out of it than Phyllis.

Women don't learn to frog breathe as readily as men, partly because they don't like the way it looks, gulping away with your mouth going through the motions of chewing gum. Phyllis resisted me. She didn't want to learn. It seemed that frog breathing was being forced on her because she had not yet been able to go and she was getting too many colds.

I frog breathed the whole of the two hours I was with her. I had only worn the chest piece to show her what it was like to take it off and be without its security, but she was too afraid to try. She wouldn't talk and wouldn't trust me. I went back to the hospital a couple of times to try again, but she never learned.

The last time I went, I heard some shocking news about David Hollingsworth, the good-looking young man with the solemn Grant Wood parents, who had been my first roommate on White Twelve. I was always envious of him because he had progressed much faster than I had, and was the first of the polio patients to leave the iron lung for a rocking bed.

I had pictured him cured, walking about, strong and handsome, but apparently they had pushed him ahead too fast. He had an epileptic seizure and lost his sight and was now in a chronic hospital where, I was to hear later, he died.

Poor David. My slow progress had outdistanced him in the end. When I got home, I told my own little David the story of the tortoise and the hare.

My son spent a lot of time with me. He loved to talk and ask questions, and when he started school, he brought his friends home to see me.

I worried because David and Susie's childhood was so different from mine. I had been king of the hill, with my mother and grandmother doing everything they could to please me, my father, my best friend, taking me around with him to see his friends and business associates, and my Uncle Hy teaching me so tirelessly how life was to be lived. I felt useless as a parent. The nearest I could get to going out with my children was to sit in my chair on the lawn and watch them play, telling David how to throw a ball or swing a baseball bat instead of showing him.

Once when he was chatting to me casually, he said, "I remember, Daddy, when you were alive, you used to take me to the swings . . ."

Dottie and I laughed and then wished we hadn't, because it startled him. He knew what he meant.

He adapted himself quite contentedly to the way things were. He developed a strong sensitivity toward my wheelchair. It was an extension of me, and when I wasn't in it, he would fondle it, stroking the back and leaning his head lovingly against it, like a dog lying on his master's slippers.

My children were so sweet, and I was so rottenly jealous and competitive and possessive of Dottie, who was trying to take care of all three of us. I would do everything I could to keep her within range, make up all kinds of reasons and ex-

101

cuses to call her back when she was just going out with David and Susie, fake a cold or start to choke to keep her at home when they planned to go to the circus, sulk if she spent too long upstairs reading to them when they went to bed.

Craziness, as I look back on it now, but I suppose I was a bit crazy—crazy with the fear of losing her, of being abandoned, of dying because she wasn't there to help me.

At the point when I began to call her Mommy, David and Susie, who were seven and five, began to call her Dottie.

My God, I thought in my saner moments, what is this doing to our marriage? What is it doing to our children?

David

It didn't do me any harm. In fact, the other way around. It was a terrible loss for my father and mother, but for me, as a child, it was mostly gains.

I never thought it was peculiar to have a paralyzed father who lived on a rocking bed to keep breathing. I was only two when he got polio, so this was all I could ever remember. A child's philosophy and understanding of life depend on what's around him, so the way my father was, that was normal to me. That was the way my life was. To me, it was abnormal that other kids could go to football games or skating or swimming with their fathers, and even though I saw how differently they lived, this was my normal. This was my father. I'd come home from school every day, and he was there—my father, the man I talked to.

This was one of the gains. He was always there. Because he was home all the time and so accessible, we formed a much closer bond than most sons and fathers do. I didn't have a father who went to work every morning and came home late and went away on business trips and was usually too busy for me, either with work or sports or jobs around the house. I had a father who always had time to talk to me.

In those days, his room was what had been the dining room, right in the middle of the house. It was on the way to everywhere, especially the kitchen. He knew how many times I went to the ice box. And I could never just walk through the room and ignore him, as you would if your father were sitting there reading the paper or working at a desk or watching television.

He was stuck there, poor guy. It wasn't exactly guilt I felt, but a sort of responsibility. I could never come home without going in there first. I could never leave the house without going in to say good-bye to him. I'd be in the hall with my coat on, and something would tell me, "Go back into the room, say where you're going and what you're going to do." Then when I was in there, I'd feel odd, because I was going to walk out and he wasn't, and there was nothing he could do about it, so I'd stay longer and try to think of things to talk about. Sometimes up in my room, I'd think, "I've got to leave the house in fifteen minutes, so I'd better go downstairs now, because it's going to take me fifteen minutes to say good-bye to Dad."

Most kids just run out. I planned my life differently. I was athletic, as he had been. When it was warm enough, he got out on the lawn in the sun, which he loved, and told me how to handle a bat or a baseball. He watched me try to put a basketball into the hoop, and he would say, "Go get a golf club. Let's see your swing." He couldn't do any of it himself, but he loved to watch me.

That was one of the adjustments he made and has been making all these years. His mental life is his own, but physically he has to live vicariously through other people.

I was always hearing people say, "Lou is so amazing, such an inspiration." That took hold of my mind, and I thought, "I must have this pretty amazing father." So I'd say to friends at school, "Come on over and meet my father. He's an amazing guy. We can talk to him." I never heard that *their* fathers were amazing or inspirational. I never met their fathers. They were never home.

My friends were intrigued when they saw him on the rocking bed, but they weren't put off by it. There were grown-ups who came to see him when he was first home who would say, "Oh my God, we can't come any more, because we can't bear to see you this way after knowing what you were like."

Children aren't like that. Their usual reaction is curiosity. They were fascinated by the apparatus and the situation, and they came back again because my dad was fun and good company and they liked to be with him.

I don't remember being disappointed or throwing a tantrum if we were all ready to go out and there was a problem with Dad, and we couldn't go. Often, things had to be cancelled. That was the way it was. Still is. If I'm busy with something and Dad says, "I need my hip moved," I drop whatever I'm doing and move his hip. His comfort has to come first, because he can't make himself comfortable. He can't scratch an itch, and he's always in pain. Always.

I don't remember resenting my mother's being too busy to have much time for me when I was little. I think she lost a lot more than we did, because she couldn't be the kind of all-caring, available mother she'd like to have been. I never had heart-to-heart talks with her, like I did with my father. My talks with Mom were usually about what I'd done wrong. She was tough. She did all the disciplining, because she had to. To Susie and me, she was the man of the house.

She made most of the decisions. When Dad gave advice, his style was to hedge. He thought about it and talked around the question and then said, "Why don't you do A *and* B, and then you've got both of them covered?" Whereas my mother would say at once, "Do B."

She was always frantically busy running the house, taking care of him, supervising the various attendants who came and went, doing everything she could to help him with the business. If I had a problem, I was more likely to discuss it with Dad. Then Mom would come in at the end and give us both the answer.

Most little kids don't know much about what's going on with their parents, but I was always aware of how difficult it was for her. I slept in the room above hers and knew how often he buzzed for her at night. Sometimes she was so tired, she slept through it, so I went down. I could do basic things for him. I sat up on a high stool or stood on the running board of the bed and did the best I could.

I wanted to help. Knowing what my mother was going through, I always felt I ought to say, "What can I do?" while still really wanting to be a child and say, "I'd rather go out and play," which I usually did anyway.

But I wanted them to know I was there if they needed me. I'd say, "If you want, I can get up at night so Mom can sleep," and they'd say, "Thanks, David," but they only asked me in an emergency.

They were juggling with a dilemma: they wanted us to help, but felt guilty if we did. That is, they wanted us to *want* to, but they were afraid that making us help would have a bad effect on us, and we wouldn't grow up normal.

You see how often the word "normal" crops up? Maybe people whose situation is abnormal are the only ones who actually think about being "normal." What is normal anyway? I don't know. Everybody has their own problems, but I guess not as immediate as ours.

My mother and father try to make the household function normally, but they really can't, because of the nature of the situation. Part of their grit is in never accepting the situation, so that my father doesn't really think of himself as a man with a handicap. I once asked him how he feels when another handicapped person comes into his room. Does he react to that easily?

"No," he said. "It bothers the hell out of me."

Once when I was about six, he switched off the motor of the bed with his head, because he wanted to be macho and show he could get along without it, by frog breathing. But he was getting exhausted, and his head had moved away from the switch and the call buzzer.

He looked at me. He was terribly distressed and starting to choke, but he managed to whisper, "You've got to get the bed on."

I couldn't reach the switch, so I went and got my mother's yardstick and turned the bed on with that.

He was proud as hell, but to me, I had only found the answer to a problem. I've always felt that I could handle a lot on my own. I must get it from my mother. I was the first kid I knew who was allowed to take the subway into Boston by myself. Unlike most families we knew, the children weren't the center of attention in our house. Dad was.

Being more responsible than most kids my age helped me to get along better with people older than myself. Most of my friends were older than me, and I got along well with my parents' friends, like Alan and Milt, who took me around with them because my father couldn't. They were great. I grew up among people who bent over backwards to do things for my father. That made me more sensitive to other people's needs, and it made me think, "This is why everybody says it's so important to have friends, because they knock themselves out to help you all the time."

It showed me how things ought to be between people, and when I grew up, it was a shock to find out that friendship isn't always like that.

Those were some of the gains for me when I was a boy. People may have been sorry for me, but I thought I was lucky, because I had this amazing man who was my father, and he was always there, and we were very, very close. I really loved him.

Susie

When I was small, I wasn't aware that there was any difference between us and everybody else.

I didn't talk about my father to anyone at school. Other kids, after all, never talked about their fathers, or what they were like or what they did. Sometimes I took friends home who hadn't been told what to expect, and one girl was so scared by the bed that she ran out of the room and down the street. She couldn't take it. Most people might feel funny for five minutes, but my father would put them at their ease, and they'd forget he was rocking.

I didn't bring many friends home when I was very young. I didn't want to, and it wasn't encouraged, because we made too much noise and got in the way. My brother would use Dad as bait, as a way to gain a new friendship, but I waited a long time before I risked bringing a friend home.

My best friend lived across the street from us anyway, so I was in her house all the time. I spent a lot of time with my grandmother and as much as I could with my mother. My father . . . he was just there.

I don't remember resenting my mother's being so busy with him. It had always been like that. I accepted the fact that any time we made plans to go somewhere, it was always "We'll have to see how Daddy is. If he doesn't feel good, we might not be able to go."

Whether it was just a shopping trip or a treat like the circus or the rodeo—my grandfather was manager of a chain of movie theaters and could always get us free seats for Boston Garden—there was always this reservation: maybe we can't go.

We had a maid in those days. Thursday was her day off, so we went out for supper. We had to eat about a quarter of four, the earliest you could get served, and rush through the meal so my mother could be back at five to help the night attendant. Finally, David and I asked, "Why not tell the night guy to come at five thirty?" Brilliant.

Since we could never go for holiday or birthday outings as a family, our outings were at home: parties, games, special cookouts. It meant more work for my mother—she'd cook for days in between doing everything else—but as I see it now, it did bring us close as a family. Even when I was quite young, I realized we were working together as a team, to overcome what had happened to Daddy.

My parents wanted to bring us up as normal children, and they wanted me to be independent and do things for myself. They made me read a lot at home and write book reports for them. Then my mother began to worry that I stayed in my room too much, so on days when I got out of school early, she made me call up people I hardly knew, friends of theirs whose children didn't even go to school with me, and try to arrange to do something with them.

I've always known her as the dominant one. What she says goes. She told me that when they were first married, she wasn't like that at all. With Dad to lean on, she was shy and hesitant, but she's changed a lot because she had to. She's so bright anyway, I don't think she'd have stayed in the background, even if he hadn't gotten sick.

I went to ballet classes, and I used to dance a lot. My father loved to watch me dance. We used to put Herb Alpert and the Tijuana Brass on the phonograph, and I would dance for him in my black leotard and pink tights. He had been a great dancer in his time, "the dance King," he told me. "They cleared the floor to watch me." I know he was envious of his friends who could still dance, but not of me.

"You're the one who's carrying it on for me," he'd say, and it made him happy to watch me. When he got into his new room with more space, he'd call me in, and sometimes he'd be looking so sad and he'd say, "I need you, Susie. Come and dance for me."

nine

As time went on and the years of my illness went by, the trips we took became more and more difficult. Instead of getting used to the bus, I became more frightened of it. I was a nervous wreck before, during, and after each trip, and I began to realize that I was running myself into big trouble, trying too hard to be normal, stretching myself to the limit to prove what I could do.

Other polio patients were mobile, more or less, according to their condition, and so I must be more mobile, go a bit farther, do a bit more, frog breathe for longer than anyone else.

Because a lot of people came to see me and I went to their houses, I was getting too many colds. Other people can be mildly embarrassed at parties by a coughing fit. Without enough breath to cough properly, I was often mortified at parties by getting choking fits, which embarrassed Dottie too, as she had to push my chest to get rid of the suffocating mucus.

I was still smoking at this time, if you can believe anybody could be so idiotic. I was nervous, and it was something to do, and neither the doctors nor Dottie had ever tried to stop me. I was so down and out already, they figured, how much more could I hurt myself?

Somebody, sometimes a guest at a party, had to light the cigarette and put it in my mouth for a puff and then take it out. I can't think why they cooperated, when the smoke was making me cough feebly and threatened to choke me. I had burns in the front of all my sweaters from people dropping ashes onto me. If I didn't choke to death, I'm surprised I didn't immolate myself before Frank Austen finally made me give up smoking.

When I had a cold, it was hell for me and hell for whoever was taking care of me. In the morning, the first bite of breakfast would usually stimulate the flow of mucus. We stopped the bed and Dottie or the attendant pushed on my diaphragm while I frog breathed, trying to synchronize the two. If that didn't work, they had to turn me over and pound on my back, which made frog breathing very difficult, and then turn me on my back and start pushing my chest again, an exhausting business for both pusher and pushee.

Breakfast could take up to two hours, grabbing bites between pushes. I would be all right for a while, then—boom!— off went the choking again, into another cycle of pounding, pushing, coughing, pounding, pushing, coughing. I have worn out three people during one cold, rotating to push me, and except for catnaps, I might be awake seventy-two hours.

The rocking bed and the chest respirator were not strong enough to breathe me through a heavy cold. If all else failed, I had to be admitted to Children's Hospital for a spell in the iron lung again.

I would be in the orthopedic section, and the children there were an example and an inspiration to me. How they could take pain! Many of them had terrible deformities. Some were in body casts, some recovering from massive operations to straighten a spine or shorten a leg to match the other one shortened by polio. The leukemia patients were on the next floor. When I talked to them in the elevator, I knew that some of them were children to whom I might be saying good-bye.

Their courage helped me to bear my own ordeals. I hated having to go back into the iron lung, that giant tin can with portholes in which I had suffered so much at the beginning of my illness. It was a regression to those terrible early days of fear and horror. On the rocking bed and in the wheelchair, I could at least see some of the world and be a part of other people's lives. Retreating to the iron lung was being thrown back into solitary confinement.

Dottie came as often as possible, and when she wasn't there, my dear Elaine always came in to comfort me and cheer me up. Our high school friendship had grown into genuine love and admiration. I could talk to her about anything, and so could some of the other patients, as she moved about the ward among them, asking the right questions, knowing what to say to make them feel good and when to keep quiet and listen.

Although the hospital was the place for me when I couldn't breathe through a cold, these readmissions set me back. Instead of getting better, which I was supposed to do, more things seemed to go wrong with me. The severe anemia for which I had to have blood transfusions at the hospital turned out to be caused by a bleeding duodenal ulcer, the origin of which was undoubtedly psychosomatic.

Frustration and stress were playing hell with me. Most people have some way to relieve frustration and anger. They can yell, shake their fists, throw things at the wall, kick the tires of their car, kick the cat, grab something out of the refrigerator, pour a drink, slam out of the house, or go for a run on the beach.

I couldn't do any of those things, and so when I was frustrated and upset, it turned inward and played havoc with my system. Stupid little things could add up to a lot of pressure. Dottie would start to bring me a urinal, and the phone or the doorbell would ring. She would answer, and I'd be left needing to pee. I'd ask the attendant to turn a page on my reading rack and have to wait while he took a look at the book himself. People would change the television channel without asking me if I was watching. That can happen to anybody, but anybody else can get up and switch it back on.

No matter what time we ate, I would take one bite of supper and Dottie's mother would call. It was not her fault, because we never ate at the same time. And it was not the children's fault that they made so much noise nor the deliverymen's that they came in and out. Nor was it Dottie's that she had a million things to do besides take care of me. But it was all building on my unrelenting pain. After a while, the pressure mounted and a valve exploded into defeating emotional and physical symptoms like anxiety and hostility and headaches and high blood pressure and the ulcer, and more pain in new places.

Even my old standby accomplishment, frog breathing, was no longer the unfailing key to freedom that it had been. Overdoing it, trying to be normal, taking too many trips away from the house, I had pushed myself too hard with it instead of using the respirator. Frog breathing was often such a great effort that I could no longer trust it to see me through whatever happened.

Then I heard a shocking story that set me back even farther in my frog-breathing career.

I'm not sure if it was a true story or some sort of myth of the kind that does float around in hospitals.

George Brady, a polio patient whom I had known in the rehab center, had learned to be an expert frog breather, as I had. He had married one of the nurses, and they went out quite a lot together.

One evening in the winter, they went to the theater in Boston. It was very icy weather, and when they came out, it was so cold that, while he was frog breathing, the alveoli in his lungs began to freeze up, and what little breath he could gulp down literally froze within him. He struggled for air, his wife panicked, and he died.

Whether that was true or not, in the mood I was in, I imagined that happening to me. Out without a respirator, frog breathing would fail me, and I would die in a storm of icy wind and snow.

I had enough fears about going out before I heard that tragic cautionary tale. Now I couldn't get out of my mind the picture of poor George struggling and suffering on a street in downtown Boston. Each time we went out, I told myself, "This is it. This is the day. This trip is going to be the death of me."

When I was proved wrong, that did not prevent me from having the same premonition all over again the next time. People who have hunches about plane and car crashes only remember if they were right. They forget the hundreds and thousands of times when they were sure of disaster and it never happened.

Not long after I heard about George Brady, my anemia sent me back to Children's Hospital for another blood transfusion.

While I was there, one of the maintenance men asked me, "Hear about Bert Fern?"

"He's doing pretty well, last I heard."

My old frog-breathing pal and his wife had stayed with us a couple of times. Dottie and Mary slept on the living room floor to be near us, and Bert was able to sleep in Dottie's bed in the den. Bert was tougher than me. Mary could pick up his hands and move him about quite energetically. He made me feel like a sissy, with my pain and sensitivity, but the difference was that he had lost the feeling in his sensory nerves.

"He went into radiology," I said. "Working pretty hard."

"*Was,*" the maintenance man said gloomily.

"He quit? He didn't let me know."

"Because he was dead, I guess."

"*Dead?* What happened?"

114

"Maybe he went back to work too soon and overdid it."

And gave himself a heart attack? That really scared me. I was trying to do as much work as I could, and Dr. Karlin was encouraging me, but here was this wonderful man who had lived in the next bed to me all those months at the rehab, my frog mate, one of the original brave frogateers—and he died of overwork.

Typically, as with the story of George Brady, I applied the story to myself. Was this going to happen to me?

The terrible news about Bert Fern was one of the key factors in my growing depression and withdrawal. I had already reached the point when I was almost too scared of the bus to face going out at all, and the few times I did, the effort and pain never made it worthwhile. David said in his practical way, "Well, you're going to have pain anyway, Dad, whether you're on the bed or in the chair, so you may as well enjoy some of it." But I didn't enjoy any of it. I couldn't enjoy anything. When a party was planned, it was a relief if I was too sick to go and didn't have to pretend to a lot of people that I was still amazing Lou, who didn't let paralysis get in the way of enjoying his social life.

One of my mother's proud rules had always been that, when something is wrong, you "make a bluff" and never let the outside world suspect. Well, I was sick of making a bluff. I didn't want to go to parties anymore.

I had to go to the Bar Mitzvah of Alan and Natalie's son, whose sixth birthday party had been my last appearance on legs before I got polio. It was a lavish affair in June 1964. They had a big tent up in the garden, and I sat in my wheelchair in a space between the tent and the house and watched the people dancing.

In my day, when I was in top form and my tireless legs had a life of their own, the other dancers used to stop and crowd round at the edge of the floor to watch me dance, at first with a variety of favored girls, then with Dottie.

Sitting out there on the grass, cut off from the music and movement, I felt for the first time a bottomless depth of regret. Envy was mild compared to the hostility I felt toward those people dancing in that tent, free from pressure and confusion and pain, and not giving a damn about mine.

When a few came up to talk to me, they seemed very uneasy, as if they too had a deeper sense of the difference between us. Some of the men tried to shake my hand, which made it worse for both of us. They tried to find the right things to say, but there was nothing I could say to them to bridge the gap between my world and theirs.

The last party I went to was for Dottie's birthday. It was at the house of one of her friends, and they held the party in a basement room off the garage so that I could go. I wished they had held it upstairs, so that I would have had an excuse not to go, but it was Dottie's birthday, and she wouldn't go without me, so I went.

I don't remember much about it, except that there were about twenty-five people, and they were going to have Chinese food. Dottie was going to feed small pieces to me with chopsticks, but before that, there were drinks and hors d'oeuvres, and she gave me a cracker and cheese, and I started to choke.

Quite often, a sip of water will work. It didn't. Dottie had to lower the back of the chair and start pushing my chest, while I grew red in the face and looked as if I were going to pass out and the guests either hovered around wanting to help, or pretended not to see me, according to their natures.

"Get me out of here!"

I was ashamed and embarrassed. Dottie took me into another part of the basement and worked on me for ten minutes, then another ten minutes, and then ten minutes more, until I begged her to take me home.

The party had been planned for weeks in her honor, and she hadn't even had dinner, let alone the birthday cake and candles, but she took me away, probably mad as hell inside, although she didn't show it. When I got home and onto the rocking bed and could breathe properly again, I said, "I don't want to go out anymore."

A few weeks later, someone else was having a birthday party, a good friend who said, "I'll be so disappointed if Lou doesn't come to my party." Dottie persuaded me to give it one more try.

Halfway there, I was overwhelmed by panic. I felt completely disoriented, shaking, sick, and dizzy. An iron band was crushing my head, and I thought I was going to throw up.

"I can't . . ."

"Take it easy, Lou." Two of our friends were with Dottie in the front of the bus. "Nothing to worry about. You'll be all right."

I made an effort to drag myself together, but I couldn't.

"Dottie, you'll have to turn around and take me home."

It was the first time I wasn't able to rise to the occasion. I had given up. At home, after Dottie had put me to bed, she sat by me and we looked at each other for a long time in silence.

Finally I said, "It's not worth it. I'm not going out anywhere, ever again."

I withdrew into the shell of my home and the safety of my rocking bed. Except for a couple of occasions, I didn't leave the house for the next fifteen years.

Dottie I was delighted when we got the van and I began to take Lou out in it. We had both been stuck in the house for too long, and this was an adventure that brought us closer to the normal life of the rest of the world.

Lou was very enthusiastic at first, and when he began to be afraid of the van, I couldn't understand it. I knew it was safe. I drove quite slowly, although it seemed fast to him. We had two of every piece of equipment in case something went wrong, but for two days before a trip, Lou would have me running around checking the van and his motors and batteries, and each time we planned to go out, it built up to a big trauma beforehand.

I found it very hard to cope with. In my family, I had never been exposed to any emotional upsets and neuroses. You got up in the morning, and you went to school or to work. If you had to do something, you did it. There were no hysterical scenes at the dinner table, with someone pushing their chair over backwards and rushing out of the room in tears. I did not understand the kind of emotional crisis that was overwhelming Lou. Because he had been competing with his children for my time since they were small, I thought that this was another thing he was creating to get attention.

I liked going out. We only went to houses of friends, and they would hover around Lou, so that I could go off and talk to other people and have a couple of drinks. It was the only social time I had away from the house, because I had no help in the evenings or at weekends. I was at home most of the time.

On that last trip when Lou begged me to turn back, it was nothing new. He had said this almost every time we went out, but I had always said, "Come on, you'll be all right" and managed to reassure him. But that built up to the point where finally I said, "All right, if you want to turn back, well then, we will."

When he told me he didn't want to go out anymore, it was almost a relief. No more anxiety attacks in the van. No more two-day traumas while he worked himself into a panic and made me check everything over and over again.

But no more enjoyable times away from the house either. We stayed home every evening, and I felt frustrated and trapped.

Since I kept asking Lou, "Are you sure you don't want to go out?" he finally said, "Maybe I will, as long as I don't have to sit up."

The old van was falling apart, so in 1970 I bought a station wagon and put a comfortable stretcher in the back for Lou, with space for all his equipment.

He thought he would go out in it. He would build himself up to the idea, but then at the last minute, there was always a reason why we couldn't go. David had his license by now and enjoyed driving the station wagon. Lou never once went out in it.

As I sank into a deepening depression, the only thing that saved me from complete disintegration was my work. I was withdrawing from the world and could only do solitary things, so I spent more time on the phone, talking to customers and suppliers, looking for new prospects, checking orders, paying endless attention to detail.

Most depressed people lose all concentration and energy, but my depression drove me into an obsessed intensity about my work and even my hobbies. My healthy self had been relaxed and casual, giving up things that didn't work out, happily taking time off with a job unfinished. My sick self was different. I stuck to things grimly, fussing and fretting about tiny details, because if I couldn't do them myself, nobody else could do them properly.

In the rehab center, where I used to make tapes from my records, I had driven everyone crazy by being such a meticulous perfectionist. Now Dottie and the attendants had to go over and over details of orders and sales. Every night I made Dottie sit down right after supper, although there were a dozen jobs she still had to do, and go through the stamp catalogs and type up the lists of my collection, until she fell asleep over the typewriter.

Although I was dependent on Dottie, she was the focus of my anger and hostility. I was jealous of her because she represented all the normal people who were free to plan their lives, go anywhere they wanted whenever they wanted, and do all the things I would never do again. Actually Dottie didn't have that freedom, but I pretended to myself that she did.

I played all those stupid testing games couples play to see who has control, and I played them unfairly. I would goad her with criticisms. Whatever she did was wrong: if she went out or if she stayed in, if she was strict with the children or spoiled them. In warm weather I had my bed out on the porch. This gave me a direct line of sight to the refrigerator door, which seemed to me to be constantly in motion, and I would want to know why.

I needed Dottie's strength and toughness, and yet I would nag at her. "Why are you so tough? Why were you so short with so and so? Why do you talk to your mother like that? Why are you so curt with me?"

Sometimes she would turn around and give it to me right back. Maybe that was what I was goading her to do.

Dottie Mostly I held my tongue and took the abuse, but Lou would needle me and needle me until I had to lash out at him. It made me feel better for a moment, but then I felt horribly guilty, because I could move and he couldn't. How could I yell at him when he had it so much worse than me?

Sometimes it seemed that he wanted me to break down and scream at him. When I did, he said he liked my spunk, but I thought he liked feeling martyred and ill-used.

In testing to see how far I could go, I went much too far

and said too much, pouring the fuel of words onto my smoldering resentment like lighter fluid onto a barbecue, until it flared into an explosion of anger between us, inescapable, searing and wounding.

If Dottie came to me with some small domestic crisis— and one of my few attributes, after all, was that I was always there to be dumped on—she would get no sympathy, but a flare-up of rage. Couldn't she understand that *my* vast interminable crisis of pain and survival was more important than whether Susie was acting up, or the man came to fix the vacuum cleaner? I expected her to put herself in my place, jump into my skin and feel what I felt. How could she compare her piddling half-ounce of problems with my ton of trouble?

Why did I give Dottie such a hard time? She was my best insurance for survival. I loved and respected her, and I needed her desperately. I was completely dependent on her because, although I had the attendants to help when she wasn't there, I could never explain to them exactly how I wanted things done. They couldn't remember details like how to boil my eggs, the sequence in which the daily nursing jobs were done, the importance of getting the sheet absolutely smooth under my back, of straightening a twisted sleeve, and keeping the cuffs of my sweater away from the sensitive skin of my hands.

Dottie knew all these things without being told, and she cared devotedly for my comfort. I should have done everything I could to hold her close, and yet it was almost as if I were trying to drive her away. One morning when she was brushing my teeth, I was so mad at her for no reason that I spat the rinse water full in her face.

She didn't say a word. She wiped her face and walked out of the room. If I had been her, I'd have kept on walking.

Because I knew she would never leave me, it was safe to take my anger out on her. I was more patient and considerate with the attendants. And with visitors and friends, I could still

121

"make a bluff" and hide my wretched state. Hank and Milt were the only ones with whom I ever let down my hair. If I had treated my friends and the attendants the way I treated my wife, they might have walked out, but if Dottie quit, she'd be quitting the marriage.

Being abandoned by Dottie was the thing I feared the most, next to death itself, which was the same thing because I knew that I would die if she left me. My mind was becoming as helpless as my body, and I was terrified to let Dottie out of my sight. If she only ran out for ten minutes to pick up something at the variety store two blocks away, I sweated and panicked through what seemed like an eternity. I imagined that the rocking bed was slowing down and I wasn't getting enough air. I lived in constant fear that I would die.

Everyone admired me as a survivor, but I was facing fear day in, day out, and I thought that it would break me. "Lou is so brave," they said, but I didn't believe I would have enough courage and strength to meet the years of pain and all the ordeals, both known and unknown, that lay ahead of me.

Although I still clung stubbornly to the idea—half-belief, half-fantasy—that I would one day get better, I had by now opened the trap door and looked into the black depths where the truth lurked, waiting for me.

One way to escape pain and the fear of death would be to embrace death. I could kill myself before this evil thing killed me, and I spent some time during the worst of my depression thinking of ways in which it might be done.

I might get someone to rig up a gun on the ceiling, with a string so that I could pull the trigger with the small movement of my left thumb. I could pay one of the attendants to give me an overdose of pills.

But even supposing I was able to swallow enough pills to kill me, Dottie had all the money. Even if I could find an excuse to get some out of her, I couldn't pay my executioner after he'd done it, and if I paid him before, he might take the money and not give me the pills.

I played with the idea of suicide, but I don't think I gave it really serious consideration. Although I hated my life and I was filled with bitterness and anger and guilt about that anger and about letting Dottie down so badly in our marriage, I still wanted to see the end of this game.

Killing myself would be more difficult than living.

ten

Dottie It took me a while to realize that Lou's emotional problems were as real as his physical sickness, but by this time it had become obvious to me and to everyone around us that he was in a real crisis, and something had to be done.

He was quite unlike his old self, very negative about everything and very demanding and tyrannical. Any time David or Susie wanted me, Lou wanted me too, always with a better reason. "They can take care of themselves, and I can't." If we made plans to do anything, Lou would stage a choking spell, just like he used to when they were small. I couldn't talk uninterrupted for two minutes on the phone, and if I went out shopping, I was grilled beforehand: "Where are you going? Why? What time will you be back?" And grilled afterward: "Why are you so late?"

The children were getting fed up, I felt suffocated, and Lou was in despair.

Elaine's Uncle Sid was a psychiatrist, and she asked him to come over and talk to Lou. He agreed that he desperately needed help, but he didn't think he was the one to give it, since he knew both of us quite well and felt too personally involved.

I wasn't sure that I wanted a psychiatrist anyway. I remembered Howard Blaine in his classy tweed jacket at the rehab center. I had made my peace with him, but he wasn't much help, although he did get me to see one important truth, that I was blaming everyone else for what I was going through.

Uncle Sid recommended a few other therapists, but I didn't like any of them. One lit up a cigar by my bed and blew smoke in my face. He was mostly interested in prison inmates, and perhaps that was why he wanted to treat me. He thought I was in jail, and I must admit there have been times when I've agreed with him.

Finally, after I was ready to give up and stay submerged in my pit of depression, we found Ed Payne, a doctor who had worked with disabled people, although he had never had a polio patient. He and I liked each other from the beginning, and we have been friends ever since. He is a tall, relaxed, peaceful man, with a face that is both strong and gentle. He came to me about once a week, and the long, hard work of discovery began.

The first hope that he was able to give me was the reassurance that the feelings and behavior I hated came from my condition, not my personality. In other words, *it wasn't my fault*. I wasn't a total failure. I had done pretty well, all things considered, because my basic personality was outgoing and optimistic. Psychologically healthy, Dr. Payne called me, and that had saved me from being absolutely wiped out.

The central core of the situation was, and still is, that, since I couldn't move or breathe by myself, I was totally dependent. Dr. Payne had done some scuba diving, so he could appreciate what it meant to have to rely on a machine to breathe you and the fear of what will happen if it breaks down.

He could see that fear, because we first met in the fall of 1964 during the hurricane season. I listened to all the weather reports. If I heard of a possible storm starting in the Caribbean, I would go into a panic that it might move up the coast and knock out my electrical power. The generator would fail, frog

125

breathing couldn't hold me, and I would die horribly, struggling for air.

We did not exactly discover anything I had never known, but he helped me to bring to the surface things I had obscurely sensed and shoved to the back of my mind. As we examined them honestly, they began to lose some of their terror.

I had to look at the truth that I was as dependent as a newborn infant—more dependent, in fact, because an infant can move and has some control over his body.

A small baby is all self-centered needs, which the world exists to satisfy. He cannot possibly imagine anyone else's point of view, and those who take care of him are there only for him, to answer his demands *instantly*.

I was focusing my needs and my dependence more on Dottie than on anyone else because I loved her, and she was the one person who really loved me. The attendants took care of me because they were paid, and they didn't do it nearly as well as she did. I wanted Dottie, but the selfish temptation to put the whole burden on her involved me in a constant struggle with myself in which there was no way to win.

My leg's uncomfortable, but Dottie's busy. How long do I wait before I call her to move it . . .? Here I am suffering pain, because I don't want to impose on her and perhaps make her angry. So dammit (I'm working up my own anger now), here I'm having to suffer the torments of hell, while she can move round the kitchen and run water and bang pans about, and run up and downstairs, and go out and drive a car, and I'm stuck on this bed in agony, because she doesn't want to be burdened with me.

Dottie had never indicated that she didn't want the burden, but it was easy for me to torture myself into this kind of thing.

With Dr. Payne, I took the risk of letting myself see that maybe I wanted Dottie to suffer, too. Because she appeared to take the whole situation in stride—paralyzed husband, small children, attendants who came and went, house full of people—I would start a complaint or an argument just to goad her. She was wise. Usually she kept silent, and that drove me crazy. The few times when she boiled over and screamed at me, I felt better afterward, like a child who has finally driven his patient mother to smack him.

Better to yell at me than leave me. I had to stay here. I had no choice, but she could either stay or go. My helpless terror of abandonment was another aspect of my second childhood.

A woman who has a baby is tied to him for the first few years, and then he begins to grow up and do things for himself, and she gradually becomes more free; but for Dottie, having me was like having a permanent baby.

As I became more depressed and anxious and restricted her more, her natural exasperation at my self-centered demands increased my infantile rage. To the baby, the mother is the universe, the source of everything good, but also of everything bad—frustrations, denials, disappointments. Small children can be angels with grandparents and babysitters, but give their mothers pure hell. Mothers don't walk out, but Dottie might.

These were the things I struggled with: helplessness, dependence, anger, fear of abandonment.

"Let's face it," Dr. Payne said calmly once. "The situation stinks."

"It always will."

"So you face that and accept it, and do the best you can with it."

Slowly, very slowly, I got the courage to talk honestly to Dr. Payne about my fear and anxiety and about the anger that made me feel so guilty. I wasn't being asked to give up the anger but to take it out and look at it, and find out what was really going on.

Dr. Payne was able to show me that this was possible.

127

"Look, your anger isn't so dangerous. Clearly Dottie's not going to let you drive her away. She loves you, and she's not going to leave you."

"Most women would."

"Doesn't the fact that she's stayed prove how much she loves you?"

Over the weeks and months, we talked about my guilt and tried to get a perspective on it. The first step was to put the feelings into words and then try to change it from the kind of irrational guilt that told me I was a bad and selfish person to something that was a problem to be overcome, rather than a weapon for self-condemnation.

Anger was inevitable in my situation, and in Dottie's. I used to think sometimes that Dottie wished I were dead so that she could be free, but I learned to see that her anger was a natural human response to the restrictions of her life, not a danger sign that she didn't love me.

My journey toward peace of mind, which has taken years and is still going on, started with a seed of trust in other people—Dr. Payne, Dottie, and gradually the attendants— that grew and developed into trust in myself and the beginnings of the reconstruction of my shattered self-esteem.

I could have remained in a hospital, I could have been a useless vegetable for the rest of my life, but Dottie and I had made a decision to hold the family together, and we had done all right so far.

"You're doing a tremendous job under impossible circumstances," Dr. Payne told me. "You'll go on struggling with pain and frustration, and you'll get upset and enraged—who wouldn't—but that doesn't make you an awful person. It makes you a normal human being, better than normal, because you've done more with nothing than many people who have two arms and legs to use. You're bringing up children, making money for Dottie, keeping your old friends and making new ones, and you're enduring and surviving in a situation where most of us would have given up and gone under."

Dr. Payne and I didn't make everything magically better. My depression went on for a long time while I was in therapy, and there were many times when I slipped back into the old nightmare, but gradually I was climbing out of the pit to where I could feel my life had some value. The doctor continued to see me about once a month and then less often, and by now he is a very good and trusted friend, someone to turn to in a crisis, always available to talk on the phone or come to the house to help me get my thoughts and feelings and insecurities straightened out into some manageable shape.

When I tell him that I'm no good because I'm still difficult and savage and demanding, he reminds me that this is probably necessary for my mind and body to survive, and without it I would have surrendered to my disablement. Instead, I live as a mature human being who has kept together a marriage where there is mutual love and respect and put two children through college while lying flat on my back. I am a force in other people's lives. I have a purpose. I am worthwhile.

During this time when I was getting to know Dr. Payne, we had a young girl living in to help with the house and the children. This gave Dottie more freedom, but not from me, because I laid claim to whatever extra time she had. Although I was beginning to make some small progress in my therapy, I was still running Dottie ragged, and the day came when my good friend Hank gave it to me straight in the face.

He had found Dottie crying one day when she was exhausted. "Don't say anything," she begged, but he said it.

"If Dottie cracks up, you crack up, Lou. You have to give her some freedom, or she won't be able to stick it out with you."

Reinforced by Dr. Payne, the message was clear: To keep Dottie, I had to let her go.

I had to allow the attendants to do more for me while Dottie went out, at first for a short while in the daytime and then, when we both got up the courage, out to dinner in the evening.

It took her courage as well as mine, because she had never done any socializing by herself since we were married, and she was shy of going out alone. Secretly I hoped she would be too nervous to go, but she wasn't going to miss the chance, and since she was attractive and lively and amusing, everyone loved to have her, and she forgot her shyness and began to enjoy herself.

I stayed home with an attendant and fretted and gloomed and imagined a dozen disasters that might keep her from coming back. I would not let the attendant "put me to bed," which was what we called getting me settled for the night. Whatever time Dottie came in—eleven, twelve, sometimes one o'clock from a party—I waited "up" for her like an unsparing parent and saved up everything for her to do: bedpan, pajamas, snack, teeth, and the chest respirator, which I wore at night in those days and did not trust anyone but Dottie to put on.

As soon as she came in the door, she had to start. If she had had a couple of drinks, I'd smell it on her and begin to worry. *What is she getting into out there where I can't follow her? Who is she meeting?*

"Don't you trust me?" she would ask when I nagged at her.

"I have to. You're my only hope. Trouble is, I don't trust men."

With the attendants, the first difficulty was finding them and then replacing them when they moved on, as they inevitably did, since the people who take this kind of job are often in a transient stage of their lives. Most of them were students

130

who needed to make extra money, and some of them were from other countries. Many had dropped out of school for a year, since it was the sixties when a whole generation of students were doing that, and either going back or never going back.

It was a weird situation for me to interview a stranger and know that, if we hired him, he would be giving me the most personal and intimate care, this guy I had never seen before in my life. I had always been a modest man, and I surprised myself by finding out how quickly I gave up all modesty and how much easier life is when you can do that.

It took a lot of patience to train each new person. Dottie taught them everything that had to be done, but it took a long time for me to get them to understand what I needed and the subtleties of exactly how it had to be done. It was so hard to explain, over and over again, to people who could never care about my convenience and comfort as Dottie cared. I couldn't teach them to anticipate my needs, as she did by instinct after all these years.

She and I knew that there was a certain logical sequence in which things should be done, and if someone else did them in a different order, it would seem to me that they were dumb. But if they achieved the same end, what did it matter if their logic was different from mine? While they were learning how to take care of me, I was learning tolerance. They could never be Dottie. They were themselves.

Each new attendant was afraid of me, and I was afraid of them. They were scared of making mistakes and hurting me. I was afraid of some crisis they wouldn't be ready to handle, like choking or the bed mechanism breaking down. I could talk my head off instructing them, but if they were going to learn and we were going to get to know and trust each other, I had to stop talking and just let them do it.

Once we had overcome the barrier of our mutual anxiety, I made good friends with some of them, where the chemistry

131

was right between us. They were not sure at first what they were supposed to be—nurse, companion, friend? They didn't know how to talk to me, so I had to break the ice and start talking about my ideas and feelings and asking them about themselves, as I have always had to do with new visitors who come into my room warily and treat me at first as different, until I show them that I am the same as them in all things that matter for friendship.

I still was not able to go out, and Dr. Payne didn't push me. He had helped my depression, but the phobias were still there—the fear of fire and of the loss of my electric power, and my terror of an accident in the van.

In 1966, when it was time for David's Bar Mitzvah, I had not been away from the house for about eight years. I didn't think I could possibly face this, but Dottie and the rabbi planned everything so that I could arrive at the temple at exactly the right moment in the ceremonies, just before the confirmation.

I was in a panic all the way there, but Dottie couldn't slow down because she was keeping to the timetable. When I arrived, flustered, anxious, embarrassed to be among the well-dressed crowd in my wheelchair, all our dear friends and family were there, and my beautiful young son was the star, and I was able to forget myself and calm down and concentrate on what was going on.

In spite of the mental and physical suffering, I wouldn't have missed it for anything. Dottie and I were touched almost to tears when we saw the rabbi put his arm around David and whisper in his ear some words of wisdom from teacher to student.

When it was over, I was rushed home with my breathing equipment, longing to get back to the safety of my room and my rocking bed. A day or so later, I asked David what the rabbi had said to him.

"Oh, nothing much."

"Like what?" Maybe I shouldn't have asked.

David grinned. "He told me my fly was open."

The only other time I went out during those fifteen house-bound years was when another rabbi asked me to go to a Boston hospital to see a paralyzed man who was terribly depressed and bitter and needed some hope and assurance that he could get back into life.

Stephen was a middle-aged engineer who had been active and healthy until he had broken his neck in a car crash three months before. The rescue squad got a respirator to him in time to save his life, but now, totally paralyzed like me, he saw no reason to go on struggling to live that life. He had asked for legal permission to have his life support system removed.

Dottie came with me and sat silently with the rabbi in a corner of the room. Steve was in a high hospital bed, and I sat by him in my wheelchair and looked up at him. He glanced down at me occasionally, but most of the time he didn't want to look at me. He was in much worse shape than I was, but then it wasn't long since his accident. He was breathing through a tube into his trachea with a flexible plastic hose connected to a motor plugged into the wall behind him. Because of the tracheotomy, he spoke with great difficulty in a harsh, metallic voice pitched high, like a tape recorder run too fast. I was being breathed by a bulky chest respirator, augmented by frog breathing when I talked.

I started out with small talk, asking him how he was doing, telling him that we had something in common, since we had both been at the University of Pennsylvania.

"I understand you're an engineer, so maybe when you get out of the hospital, you can think about . . . "

"No." He interrupted me abruptly and his words were like a blow between the eyes. "I know what you've done, and I admire your courage, but I don't choose to live the rest of my life like you."

"But it's still life."

"Not for me. I'm a very physical man. I like to swim and keep fit, do things around the house, fix up my car. I've been successful in my profession. OK, so now it's over. I've done everything I want in life."

"I'm physical, too. Sports was my life. Now I have to live through my mind, and I'm learning that your mind is worth much more than your body."

"I'm not putting down anything you've done," he said, although sitting below him, I could feel something coming from him that was almost like contempt. "But I don't want to have to go around looking like you."

I swallowed that, along with some breath to argue. "You don't want to try to live the best way you can?"

He shook his head. "All right for you, but I don't want it." His face was closed and aloof. *All right for you peasants . . .*

I was furious. I had chosen to live this way, to fight the paralysis and the pain and make the best I could of it because I thought this was the right choice for me and my family. The only choice, in fact. I couldn't give up.

When Steve began to talk again, in his painful robot's voice, he said, "I've asked them to pull the plug on me."

That seemed to me so unbearably cowardly and selfish that I had to ask him, "What about your wife and children?"

"I've got two kids in college and a thirteen-year-old at home. My wife's just been accepted in a master's program at Harvard, and I can't interfere with her career. I don't want her to have to wipe my ass for the rest of my life."

"What do she and the children say?"

"They agree."

"To what?"

"That my life's over."

"It doesn't need to be. Mine isn't. I'm helping Dottie to

run a business. I'm responsible for my two children. I help to support my family. Dammit, I think I'm still worth something."

"What good is your life?"

His egotistical negativism aroused my fighting spirit. In my old sports days, I always had to win. I never lost a game at home now, or a sale, if I could possibly help it.

While I was bringing up the arguments about the need to see his young son grow up, and the advantage of a paralyzed father being always there to talk, Steve's wife and teenage son walked into the room and stood listening just inside the door.

I had my back to them, and the noise of the two motors covered any sound they made, but Dottie could see them. She told me afterward that she started to say something to stop me talking about death and surrender in front of the boy, but then she thought, "His mother's there, she'll do it." But she didn't.

"Life is a gift, Steve."

"You think so." Again in the downward glance, that suspicion of contempt. "I think more about the quality of life."

"Quality is a state of mind."

"Not when you can't move, not even one hand. Not when they have to suction the mucus out of you. I can't stand that."

"You could learn to frog breathe. I'll come back and teach you. Then you wouldn't have to be suctioned, and part of the time you could be free of the machine."

"The only way I'll be free of it is if they turn it off."

"I knew a man—my frog-breathing mate at the rehab hospital—he had been a pediatrician." I told him about Bert, who had switched to radiology when he couldn't be a children's doctor anymore. "I'll tell you about another patient there, a nuclear physicist. He was so angry and depressed, he wouldn't talk to me or anyone, but he ended up writing magazine articles and selling them. You could do something like

135

that, too. With your knowledge and experience, you could do research, consulting, dictate reports for other engineers."

He looked down at me without answering. I couldn't get through to him.

"Listen," I begged. "You're giving up too fast. You've only been like this for three months. You haven't given it time."

"Time enough. I've thought about it all, and none of it will work for me."

After about half an hour, I asked Dottie to take me away. I was exhausted. I couldn't talk anymore. "May I come and see you again?"

"If you want, but you're not going to make me change my mind."

Dottie turned my chair around, and it was then that I saw Steve's wife and son standing there, very quiet, by the foot of the other bed.

His wife came out to the hall with us, and when I said good-bye, she nodded to me and smiled sadly, and I thought she was telling me, "I think you're right."

"Please call us if we can help."

"Maybe she won't," I told Dottie at home, "but I'll go back anyway. I can't leave him like that." I thought about the wife and son standing there listening to him telling me that death was better than life. "Even if he was only making a grandstand play, the whole thing was so shocking, so alien to what I believe, so . . . so abhorrent. I guess I should be sympathetic, but I'm furious with him. Bert and George— they wanted so much to live, and they couldn't. They didn't have a choice. This guy has a choice, and he wants to throw the whole thing away."

I planned to go back to talk to Stephen as soon as possible. I had lost the first round because I hadn't expected his coun- terattack, but next time I'd prepare a better case. I would give him arguments he couldn't shoot down, to make him change his mind.

His wife didn't call. A week later, I was reading *The Boston Globe*. When I finished the feature I wanted to read, there was no one around to turn it over, so I idly looked at the obituaries on the same page.

Stephen was dead.

The rabbi told us that he had been granted legal permission to have his life support removed. He was given sedatives to make him less aware that he was suffocating, and the machine was turned off by an outside doctor who had never seen him before.

"But I only saw him last week. How could they make that decision so quickly?"

"They didn't, Lou. The judge's hearing was some time ago. It seems that when you saw Stephen, he already knew."

All the time I had been talking to him, knocking myself out, taking his insults, trying to help him see the value of life, all that time he *knew* what he was going to do.

Later, when I could think more calmly, I was able to accept that everyone must make their own decisions and take responsibility for what they do with their own lives. I would never understand Steve's point of view, but although I made no impact on him, he made a great impact on me.

He was committed to suicide. I was committed to life. I knew that now, absolutely. *Why? Why me? Why life? Why struggle with pain?* Through Dr. Payne and my growing understanding of my situation, I had been getting some small conditional answers to the questions I had flung at God in a panic of rage and anxiety. Now, although I had been through my own suicidal hell, Steve's terrible choice had shown me that my choice was the right one, for me.

eleven

After that we sold the old black and red van, and I stayed at home, where I felt safe. The nearest I got to a trip outside was being pushed in my wheelchair onto the porch or out to the front lawn on a sunny day. I stuck to my determination to let Dottie have more freedom, and eventually, ten years after she had driven me to the emergency room at Mass. General with a raging unknown fever, she was bold enough to take a week's vacation, and I was bold enough, or rash enough, to let her go.

Now when she goes away, I manage at home with a complicated program of daily and live-in attendants and nurses, but in those days I wasn't ready to do that, so I went back to Mary McArthur, like a dog going to a boarding kennel.

I did not try to belong there or to recapture the clubby atmosphere of the old days. I was a fish out of water, and after the first pleasure of renewing acquaintance with the few people I knew who were still there, I withdrew into the small world of my cubicle and the unfamiliar rocking bed and hardly talked to anyone.

This place that had been so secure for me before had now become a nightmare. Dottie had actually abandoned me, but I didn't want Dr. Payne to come and help me straighten out my thinking on that. I had been telling everyone how well I was doing, and a visit from a psychiatrist didn't fit in with the age-old Sternburg policy of "make a bluff."

It was depressing to see the patients here still dependent on nurses, but it made me see how lucky I was to be in my own home with Dottie to look after me and love me and the children in and out of my room all day. I was glad they didn't come at set times like the visitors here, who didn't have much to talk about because the patients were so far removed from their world.

Elaine came every day to cheer me in my kennel. When I had been agonizing all night about Dottie, it was wonderful to see Elaine in the morning, with her smiling cat's eyes and fluid, humorous mouth.

"If Dottie never comes back," I would ask her, "will I have to stay here forever?"

"Who says she's not coming back?"

"I do. I wouldn't, if I were her. Sometimes I lie here and wait and wait for you to come"—I was good at piling on the agony for Elaine—"and I start thinking that I won't ever see her again."

"And when you do"—Elaine wouldn't encourage wallowing—"it'll be so great, because you'll appreciate her all the more."

She was right. When Dottie came home, all the small resentments and frustrations faded to nothing before the dazzle of joy of her being such a marvelous, fascinating, entertaining, and loving woman, and the best thing that ever came into my life. Other husbands told me that separation brought the same fresh awareness to their marriage, so it was good to be reminded that I was normal.

Sometimes when I fall morbidly into analyzing what's wrong with me, I upgrade it to what's different about me, and then I can upgrade that into: emotionally, nothing. Everyone is a mixture of confidence and self-doubt. I've come to the conclusion that I'm not any different from other people, except that I'm rocking up and down, and they're not.

Dottie

My friend Dodo and I decided to go to Florida. I would stay six days, and then her husband would come down to meet her there. We planned the trip for months. Lou's doctor put him back into the rehab hospital, where they would care for him and give him a good checkup, which he hadn't had in a while.

It was very strange. I was leaving the children who were used to having us both around all the time. They would stay at home with a sitter, but there was the normal anxiety about whether they were getting enough love and care.

While I was away, I didn't call Lou because he couldn't talk on the phone in the ward, but I thought of home constantly. I felt guilty to be basking in the sun while other people suffered because I wasn't there. Dodo and I laughed a lot and ate at crazy hours and stayed up half the night and slept in the daytime, anything to break the rigorous home routine. I tried to relax, but it was hard, because I was convinced the family and the attendants couldn't get along without me.

When I came home, I was amazed to find that the change had been relaxing for them, too. They had all survived, although they had saved up strings of complaints for me. This still happens whenever I come back from a trip. Like most wives, I haven't even taken off my coat before the bad news starts, but now I expect the complaints and let them roll off my back. I go away for longer trips, ten days to two weeks, and can start relaxing the minute I step out of my front door. I don't call home, because it upsets Lou more if he hears my voice.

Change is good for all of us. Lou appreciates me more, and I miss his companionship when I'm away and am reminded of what it means to me. We have a lot to share when I come home, and we are both learning to make better use of our vacations. Unfortunately, he never gets a vacation from routine and pain.

After a week in the rehab center without doing any work, I was glad to get back to our business, and I put more energy into expanding my contacts on the phone to keep in touch with old customers and get more new ones.

A group of my friends met in my room from time to time to guide me. They decided that Dot Sales had to do more than just sell woven labels, because one day before I knew it the children would be ready to go to college, and we would need more money.

Could I become a travel agent without traveling? Could I get into the brokerage business or learn paralegal work?

"Electrical supplies," someone said. "They can be sold over the phone."

"Like labels," someone else said. "Labels, size tags, washing instructions—those are paper tags, and while you're in the tag business, you could get into wrapping paper, shopping bags, corrugated boxes . . ."

Eventually we added every kind of paper used in business. Copy paper led to pencils and paper clips and all kinds of small office essentials, and with the computer boom, we extended our line to data product supplies. The trick has been to stay away from the main products and concentrate on items that are small, easily manufactured and shipped, and need repeat orders. They are necessary but not vital to production, so it doesn't matter that I can't make visits. Our products can be sold by me anywhere in the country that is reachable by phone.

All our new companies already had salesmen on the road. Most of them were willing to team up with me and split the commission because I gave them my contacts, which were strong enough to assure them of being well received. That's fifty percent of the game for a salesman.

The old-boy network I knew through our families and people I had been with at college or already knew through business led me into new and wider contacts. I tried not to trade

141

on being paralyzed. Unless a purchasing agent asked me out-right why I wasn't calling on him in person, I never told him that I was phoning from my rocking bed respirator.

My contacts knew, but my condition didn't guarantee a sale. One man told me that business and friendship didn't mix, which may be true, but it could also have been an excuse not to help.

Another guy upset me by saying coolly, "I don't give charity to cripples."

I screamed at him over the phone, which never works, because my air runs out and I can't keep it up.

What I did trade on were my skills as a salesman and the old sound principles that Dottie's father had taught me years before. For a short, disastrous time I had worked at his wom-en's clothing store in Framingham, until I walked out after a fight, telling him to take his store and shove it. The next time I spoke to him was when he came to the polio ward at Mass. General. I'm told we both apologized, although I was too ill to remember, and we became good friends.

"Pay attention to every detail," Nat Dershowitz used to say. "Anticipate what people want, write everything down, don't trust your memory, and never forget, Louis, never for-get, the customer is king."

When my business day was over, I kept as busy as possible by developing my hobbies. I was determined not to vegetate in a rut of pain. I continued the stamp collection I had started with Dottie with a special collection of stamps that commem-orated artists and composers, so I could learn something val-uable at the same time.

As a child, I had lived near the Museum of Fine Arts, and I used to wander over there occasionally and marvel at the colors and the miracle of a flat painting on the wall being somehow three dimensional and alive so that, instead of just looking at it, you could enter into it. Stamps started me reading about the great artists who created these miracles, and the musicians series started me recording classical music with some of the attendants, and reading biographies of the composers and everything that was written on the album covers.

Then Bob Kane turned up to work for me, a tall, slim, young married teacher with sandy hair and fair skin, very relaxed and slow moving. He wasn't the world's best nurse, but in his own time he got around to making the best contribution to my life of any attendant so far.

He taught me to play chess.

So that I could see the game, he built a four-by-three-foot pegboard with a hook on very square. He designed thick cardboard pieces like modern chess figures, painted them white and black, and cut them out with holes at the top for rings to hang on the hooks. When we played, the board stood against the back of a chair or on the half open doors of one of the cabinets in my room.

Patiently he taught me. I was fascinated. I wanted to play constantly. Even though I knew Bob had been a champion chess player in the service, I was determined to beat him, and when I did finally take a game months later, I dreamed about it every night for a week.

If I was obsessive about my stamps, I was absolutely consumed by chess. Dottie wouldn't learn to play with me because she wanted me to be enjoying something with someone else. Bob and I always played chess when she was out, and the intriguing game not only took my mind away from pain but also away from the fear and uncertainty that still plagued me when she wasn't there.

I played chess by mail with people I knew, which is a bit slow for my impatient soul, but it keeps you thinking back and forth for three months, which is about how long it took us to finish a game. When Bob left, I taught his replacement, the Japanese student Hisashi, to play, and he got so good at it that he began to win our games very soon and went on to beat some top-flight players in the area, which for me was the next best thing to beating them myself.

The next improvement in my life came in 1964. The converted dining room was getting unbearably crowded, and because of the growth of her business, Dottie was able to make a down payment on a loan to build me a room of my own at the back of the house.

We talked to friends who were architects and designers and told them all the marvelous things we wanted, and then inhibited them by telling them how much we could pay—and we weren't even sure that we could pay that. I had to make a tactful check with our largest customer to assure myself that his business was in good shape, since the mortgage payments might depend on him.

The new room was designed as a two-story addition, with a high cathedral ceiling. In the dining room, I was rocking up toward a seven-foot ceiling, and the bed dominated the confined space of the room. The new room is large enough to put the bed in proportion, and the high vaulted ceiling, with lights set into hollow cross beams to reflect upwards, gives a beautiful sense of space and light. The room was also designed as a place for visitors, with plenty of comfortable places to sit, and when we have a party, twenty people can be standing around talking to me or each other without crowding.

Windows on two sides bring me into closer contact with the garden, the trees, and the sky. There is a bay window with a wide sill near my bed, where Dottie sits when she talks to me. The two inside walls have bookcases and shelves, with a counter for the television and stereo and my fish tank and big cabinets below to keep all the bedding and nursing paraphernalia out of the way.

Everyone knew a builder, and he was always "the only

builder." We got several bids, and luckily one of the lowest was from the man we liked the best. We had known as soon as he walked into the room, knowledgeable, enthusiastic, friendly, that he was for us.

Lou Wolk had been ill, and we found out later that he had been very depressed and sorry for himself. He told us that, when he came into my room and saw me, he knew his problems were trivial. This was his first job since his illness, and the project was as good for him as it was for me. He would spend hours with me explaining the plans and lovingly describing each piece of wood and its purpose. He was an artist, not just a builder. This dear man and his wife Lillian became part of our family and our daily lives, and the six months of hell that people had promised us with workmen in the house turned out to be six months of excitement and pleasure.

Lou covered the window near my bed with a swinging wooden flap, so that I could shut myself away from the work out there or open it and watch my new room growing, which was what I wanted to do most of the time. As soon as the room was framed and a rough floor put in, Louie cut a doorway through to my room so I could go into the new room in my wheelchair. Dottie and I spent every weekend sitting out there, having picnic lunches and planning every detail of how the room would be finished and decorated. By the time it was done, it was already my home.

Rocking away by the big bay window, I spent hours communing with my little corner of nature. Goldfinches and cardinals and jays came to the bird feeder. The trees and bushes were leafing out into the full rich green of summer. On my fortieth birthday, my friends planted a young oak tree outside my window to replace a diseased Dutch elm that was cut down when Louie built the room. For twenty years, I've watched that growing tree go through its cycle of adapting to the changing seasons. I feel a great affinity to it, because that oak and I have both survived by knowing how to adapt.

145

When I was a healthy young man, I loved the outdoors, and I learned the fascination of the unchangeable, everchanging sea during my thousands of Pacific miles with the navy, but I had never had time to study and contemplate. A leaf was just a leaf. I'd hardly given it a glance. Now, while I lay and watched a single leaf unfold, I began to understand some of the complicated development from seed to open leaf and flower, a microcosm of the infinitely more complex processes of man's body and brain.

O. Henry wrote a short story about a very young bedridden girl who watches a magic tree outside her window for inspiration. She loves the spring when the tree comes to life and dreads the coming of winter when its leaves must drop, because she has a premonition that when the last leaf falls she will die.

There always seems to be one dried-up leaf that hangs on through each winter, but one vicious stormy night, when the girl is very ill, that last leaf is ripped from the tree. Knowing her fear, her neighbor, an old artist, goes out into the howling snowstorm and paints a leaf on the brick wall opposite her window. When she wakes and opens the curtains in the morning, she believes that her leaf is still there and finds the courage and the will to live.

But the old artist has died of exposure out there in the storm.

My oak is my magic tree. When I am depressed and in pain and wondering why I go on struggling, its presence outside my window encourages me to endure one more hour, one more day.

When Louie and his carpenters had finished my room, Dottie had some renovations done in the kitchen. In the process, the line that connected my buzzer to all points in the house was cut. This buzzer that I activate with my head is my lifeline because I haven't enough breath to call for attention or help, especially now that I am not in the middle of the house. One long signal means I'm in serious trouble. Two is for Dottie or the attendant. Three and four were for David and Susie when they lived at home.

When I'm on the bedpan, the attendant leaves me, and I buzz when I'm ready. I was on the bedpan when the carpenter cut the line. I buzzed several times, and nothing happened. I took a huge frog breath and yelled as loud as I could. Pretty soon someone would come in to see how I was. Nobody came.

A steel bedpan is a literal pain in the ass when you have only skin and bones for buttocks. Frog breathing can get very difficult under stress. The inside of my mouth parched. Pretty soon, I would cough and choke. I could see the headlines tomorrow: POLIO PATIENT DIES ON BEDPAN. It was very frightening. I tried to stay calm, but I was in increasing distress as thirty minutes went by, then forty-five . . .

When Dottie finally put her head calmly round the door and asked, "Are you all right?" I gave her hell because of the relief of seeing her.

Being farther away from the rest of the house was a risk that I took, but it was a sign of my progress toward independence, and it was worth it.

This was my own suite, where people could come to see me without disrupting the rest of the house, and now I was farther from the sounds of the front door, the children's feet on the stairs, kitchen clatter, barking dogs and motor bikes and loud voices on the street. Best of all, Dottie and I finally had complete privacy for uninterrupted conversations and for our sex life.

Spiritual closeness between Dottie and me is the heart of our relationship, but love is affirmed and strengthened by sexuality. Polio and paralysis did not affect my desire or my feeling. I was turned on easily and often, and Dottie never said no to me, however tired or distracted she was, although she did not always get physical satisfaction. She had to be the aggressor, and her pleasure was to give me pleasure and the release of energy that could engulf me with a joy and deliverance that temporarily overwhelmed pain.

I was in my new room when the great blackout of 1965 knocked out the Northeast. We ran the house on the emergency generator my father had put in for me when I first came home, and I spent those strange, deadened hours in fear. Every time the refrigerator cut in, the lights flickered, and I imagined that my bed was slowing down because the generator was failing. There is so much about fear in this story that you may think me a coward. I don't think I am, really, or I could not have made a good life out of disaster, but when you are helpless and vulnerable, you do live with fear, because so many things can go wrong over which you have no control.

One of them was Craig.

He was a Vietnam veteran from North Carolina, an athlete who came to live with us in the new apartment under my room. One afternoon when Dottie was out, he told me that the responsibility of taking care of me was too much for him.

"I'm not what you think I am," he said. "I'm not an athlete. I don't pole vault. I'm not strong. I'm freaking out. I've been in a mental hospital, and I'm scared. I won't hurt you, but I've got to talk."

He locked the two doors to my room and then did hurt me by grabbing my hand and digging his fingernails into my wrist.

"I've got to talk to you." His eyes were confused, and his voice was desperate. "You shouldn't have taken me on. I'm a nut case. I'm schizo. Once, I bit off a man's ear."

He talked to me about Vietnam, and I tried to talk to him like a friend and fellow veteran, to calm him down, but after an hour, when I asked him to unlock the door because Dottie would be back soon, he refused.

"I'm not letting her in here."

When she came home, she knocked on the door at the

other end of the short passage, which Craig had also locked. "I'm here!" I called out. "I'm here with Craig." I was afraid he might hurt me if I called for help, but I wanted to let her know that he was holding me hostage. "I don't want her in the room." He was very agitated. I didn't know whether he was going to bite off my ear, or kill me.

At last, I managed to get him calm enough to let me phone Dottie on our other number. She called Milt and asked him to come over. "But don't let her in here. I don't want to see anybody." We arranged that she could come in through the corridor, waiting after he had unlocked the door until he had escaped through the bathroom. He let go of my wrist, which was in agony, unlocked the doors, rushed out as Dottie came in, and went downstairs to his room. When Milt came, he talked to him and persuaded Craig to readmit himself to the hospital.

Dottie The greatest trauma of those times was when Lou took his first bath in the oversized tub that had been installed in the new bathroom.

Not having had a tub bath since leaving the rehab center, he had mixed feelings. He still had vivid memories of the horrors of the Hubbard tub, but he felt grimy. Bed baths were never enough.

We had hoped to copy the design of the Hubbard tub setup on a much smaller scale at home; but the overhead trolley to hold the stretcher couldn't be built under the cathedral ceiling. We had to design something else. So we wrote to several rehabilitation centers and asked around about local patients who had tubs. The answers were all discouraging. The rehab literature was for people who could use a hydraulic bath chair, and obviously this was no use to us, since Lou had lost the neck muscle control to support his head.

Then we heard of a few patients who had been braver than us and had already installed bath tubs in their homes. We asked them about the mechanics of taking a completely paralyzed, frog-breathing person out of his bed and through the bathroom door to a position over the water. Then he would be slowly submerged horizontally, but only to the point where there was absolutely no danger of drowning. We would wash him from both sides of the tub, then lift him out of the water, somehow dry him enough to make the return trip back through the door to a freshly made bed, and finish drying him front *and* back, all the while keeping him covered to protect him from a sudden chill. How would we do this so that he would end up lying on dry sheets, warm, dressed, and comfortably refreshed?

"Don't ask us," they said. Although they had bath tubs, not one of them had dared to test it. Obviously, we were on our own on this one.

Where to start? After asking around, we hit on a fellow we had both known years earlier, Buddy Hyman, an engineer designing conveyor systems for industry. Buddy could take a simple wire hanger and create all sorts of miracles in a Rube Goldberg kind of way. When we told him our problem, he grabbed it like a fish with a baited hook.

Buddy started out with old aluminum furniture from his backyard and made a stretcher to fit inside our large, old-fashioned tub on legs. He called or came around almost every day, excited about new ideas and new people whom he had involved in this project. By hook or by lifter, he was going to get Lou into the bath. He didn't know that, while I was sharing his enthusiasm, Lou had a gnawing fear in his gut about even trying any of these great ideas, let alone using them regularly. I remembered Lou's utter terror of Wellesley bath days, and I was afraid that once the challenge of figuring out the system was over, I would never be able to talk him into using it.

Finally Buddy designed a litter that hooked over the sides of the tub and had nylon ropes with hooks to attach to Lou's lifter. There was an extra wooden strip to keep the stretcher from submerging too deep—a belt as well as suspenders, we thought. The big trial day came, although Buddy had great confidence in his invention, he wanted a dry run with me as the patient. Perfection! We were ready for Lou.

In the early summer of 1964, we took our maiden voyage. I couldn't stand waiting anymore. My anxiety was worse everyday, but I had painted myself into a corner. I would be mortified if I didn't try it. I didn't want an audience to see me in a panic, so one Sunday, although Dottie and I were alone in the house, we decided to give it a whirl.

Dottie I turned on the water to fill the monstrous tub. How hot? How full? What if I screwed up and soaked Lou's mattress? Would he really go through with it once I got everything ready, the tub filled and the litter in place? My God, I didn't even know what I was doing.

Oh, my God, water again! "Sink or swim," the camp counselor had yelled, and I damn near sank. I had thought I would drown in the Hubbard tub. Now I knew I would, in my own bathroom.

Nobody was forcing me to do this, but I had to see if I could. I hated to give in. Anxiously I watched the lifter approaching my bare body. All of a sudden, I was hanging out over the floor in the nylon sling. The books on the shelves traveled past my eye. Will I ever see this bookcase, this beautiful room, again? There was a little bump as the wheels of the lifter rolled from the wooden floor to the tiles. The point of no return. I was sure the lifter would break, but as it rolled into the bathroom, the sun came through the window and passed over my face like the light of hope. When Dottie asked me, "Are you sure you want to do this?" I said, "Sure."

As I slowly descended on the stretcher, I could feel the moist heat of the water on my back. So far, so good. Dottie released the upper side hooks and lowered the hydraulic lift so that my upper torso sank into the water. I was frog breathing as fast as I could.

My God, she's going to drown me! "I'm in deep enough! I'm in deep enough! Stop!"

Dottie Stop? He's hardly in the water. It isn't even covering his knees. The whole top part of his body is above water. Should I stop or just submerge him and give him a good bath? This is a crucial event, better let him have it his way.

Where do I wash first? What's most important, seeing that he'll probably yell to get out in two seconds? Well, let's go. Jesus, the water moves when I start to wash him. It's going over his chest. It's lapping his chin. I'd better watch out.

Boot camp in the navy, jumping into water from a twelve-foot platform into an oil slick on fire and coming up outside the outer edge of the fire. That was the worst water experience until the Hubbard tub, and then again now. The waves from Dottie's washing movements brought the water almost into my mouth. How am I going to frog breathe? CRACK! The wood brace that supported my upper body let go. The stretcher

152

tilted to one side. My life didn't flash before my eyes, but I thought this was the end.

"Get me the hell out of here—fast!"

Dottie was already pumping the lifter.

Dottie My God, what was that? The safety board. How could I have been stupid enough to try this when I'm all alone in the house? I can't even call anyone because I can't leave him hanging over the water. Just pump like crazy and get him attached to the edge of the tub and let out the water. He'll never go in again after this. Oh, my God, I've blown it.

I don't remember the trip back to the bed. I remember feeling exalted because the trial was over, but also disappointed that it wasn't finished.

Dottie didn't think I'd try it again, but I thought that with better safety precautions, I could do it. So Buddy made a heavy aluminum brace which was much safer, and I began to bathe in the tub three days a week.

Dottie His skin isn't all that great now, because of years of rocking, but soaks in the tub have kept it in a condition that surprises the doctors. He looks forward to bath days now. We've had to cut it down to twice a week because the procedure takes so long and his activities and interest are so varied he can't find enough hours in the week for everything. We still don't know any other patients who bathe in a tub at home.

Four months after I moved into the new room, my beloved father died.

He came into my room one day and said, "I don't feel well,

Louis. I'm awfully tired and have these pains in my chest. I think my days are numbered."

"Come on, Dad, you're indestructible."

But he wasn't. He was overweight, he ate all the things he shouldn't that my mother loved to cook for him, and he still smoked cigars. For some years, he had felt very bitter about things that had gone wrong in his business. Television was taking people away from his movie theaters, and he was losing his power. He couldn't stand that, anymore than he had been able to stand the loss of control over what had happened to me.

Of all of us, he was the one who was least able to come to terms with my illness. When I was a child, he had told me, "Never give up." And he always believed, even more strongly than I did, that somehow, some way, something would change. He never gave up feeling and stroking my hands, to see if anything moved.

He was wearing a blue-check shirt, and he had his cigar, and he stood in my doorway before he left and asked, "Anything I can do for you, son?"

"No thanks, Dad. Take care. You'll be all right."

I never saw him again.

Uncle Hy arranged the funeral. I couldn't be there, because I wasn't going out in those days, but I wrote the eulogy for the rabbi to deliver.

At first, I wept for the irrevocable loss of this man who was my best friend. Then I began to feel peace for both of us, because I knew that our association was so strong that death could not destroy it.

twelve

In 1967, I entered the electronic age when Glenn, the son of a friend of mine, a fifteen-year-old high school student, revolutionized my life. I was using a headset so the bed no longer had to be stopped for me to use the phone. Glenn put a mechanical cellinoid switch on my telephone and then molded a plastic device with a microswitch attached to it to fit over my index and middle fingers. God has seen fit to leave me with some very small movement in my left thumb, and Glenn took God's gift and turned it to practical use. A touch of my thumb on the microswitch turns on the phone and connects me with the operators. They dial for me, and I can reach any phone in the world. The operators all know me—panel 2, jack 42—"Hi, Lou, how are you doing today?"

As far as I'm concerned, the telephone was invented by Glenn Axelrod. Later, he improved the technology by using electronics with a scanner switch, so that I could turn on not only the phone but also the television, reading light, and tape recorder.

With the phone available to me at any time, I could not only do more work; I now had some control over my environment. For the first time, the situation wasn't entirely controlling me. I was overcoming it.

Although I still had occasional relapses into the crippling inertia of depression, my mind was becoming more energetic and active. Michelangelo's *Pietà* was at the World's Fair on

Long Island, and I dictated an article about the history of Michelangelo on stamps, and sent it to a philatelic magazine. They published it, and this made me want to do more writing. The stamps themselves were getting a bit boring, and so was recording music. After the stamps had been arranged in the album, or the music had been reproduced on tape, I seldom bothered to look or listen. My blood was up for a challenge, so I thought that I would write short stories for publication in magazines, like the Michelangelo stamp article.

I started a series of stories about a woman named Belle Boyd, who was a spy for the South during the Civil War. I never submitted any of them because they seemed to me to be too contrived. Dictating is hard. If you use a tape recorder, you can't go back and correct and move your words around, and if you use a live person, you have to be terribly confident not to be inhibited by anxiety about what they will think. If they make suggestions, you could kill them, and if they say nothing, you think, "Oh God, they don't like it."

My characters were coming out like concrete blocks, so searching farther, I wrote to Brandeis University, which is not far from where we live, and asked them if they could supply me with a creative writing teacher. They sent me Ruth Stone, who helped me a lot and delighted me by being a genuine absentminded professor, wandering into my room with a serene, spaced-out smile, wearing one black shoe and one brown.

I wanted to know more about human nature in order to write better, so I asked Brandeis if I could audit a psychology course by using tapes of the lectures at home. My request was picked up by Dr. Brendan Maher, a Welsh professor who was about my age and had also been in the navy. At the end of his course on personality, he came to lunch with us and casually dropped the suggestion that I might take a regular course and get an advanced degree in psychology.

He dropped it out of the blue, and although it scared me,

I recognized it as a chance to go on with the search, which I believe is the whole point of existence on earth.

Nothing is ever enough. No one who aspires to achievement is ever entirely satisfied when they succeed. Life at the top is difficult for many reasons, and one of them is that the goal can never equal the desire. The spirit can never stand still. It must always seek and progress. It must always have something ahead.

It took two years for me to get up the courage to enter the graduate school at Brandeis and for them to work their way through the red tape necessary to admit me as a special student. I couldn't go to class, so I read and listened to the cassettes of the classes and gave my answers to tests onto tape or dictated them to Dottie on both our honors. Although I had picked up some psychology through my therapy with Ed Payne, it was unnerving to be plunged into a lot of new academic information and ideas. It was slow and difficult for me at first and I thought I was the ultra dummy of the world.

That first year, I took courses in things like personality and motivation, and I learned about the different schools of psychotherapy. I discovered Freud and became fascinated with him. Because I was more of an observer of the scene than a participant, his analytical approach made sense to me and carried my mind forward on the new adventure of dissecting and analyzing every little thing that everybody did, which further increased my growing sense of control. If you can't join 'em, understand 'em. It was a way not to be left behind by other people's lives.

After a while, I followed a sideline that combined my interest in psychology with my knowledge of sports. I had been reading about the college students drafted by the Boston Patriots, and I wondered how much money was spent scouting, choosing, and training them and how much of that money went down the tubes when a player didn't work out. Many

157

of the first round selections did not eventually make the team. If everyone's abilities were more or less the same—speed, mobility, strength—what was the difference between the guy who made it onto the team and the guy who didn't?

Psychology! That was the answer to everything for me at that moment, and I set about to develop a test that would show in advance who had the psychological tools and motivation to make it as a professional.

I had always dreamed that, when I walked again, I would win the Ben Hogan Comeback Award, named for the famous golfer who recovered from a terrible car accident in spite of prophecies that he would never walk again and went on to win the U. S. Open. While I was waiting to compete again myself, the psychology of those who were currently competing would be a way for me to get back into sports.

I read a lot, including a book on psychological testing, and saw that the criteria for an acceptable test were validity and reliability. Gino Capelletti, a friend of mine who was a professional football player, encouraged me. An attendant who was a student at Babson College talked about my project to one of his professors, John Hornaday, a professor of management and entrepreneurship who had worked with psychological tests and knew a lot about statistics.

Through Gino, we got some of the top athletes over to my house, to find out what they were really like and what they had in common. My job was to develop the concepts of the study, and John's was to get the information and turn it into workable statistics. But I did just as much talking to the athletes as he did because I loved having them around, even though my admiration couldn't help being tinged with envy of their strong bodies and the easy way they moved. When I see physical beauty and grace, it makes it harder for me to accept my useless body and the pain that keeps coming like the waves of the sea, some days angry, some days more placid, but always relentlessly advancing.

158

We started a small corporation with James St. Clair, who was Gino's and Jack Hornaday's lawyer and later to be Richard Nixon's. After the concepts of our study were developed, we heard about two men at San Diego State University who were using the same kind of test for the San Francisco 49ers and the Dallas Cowboys, after interviewing athletes from all over the world.

We sent for a copy of their study and found to our joy that we had come up with the same criteria they had. But they were only using multiple choice questions, while our test allowed for a much more subjective freedom of answer. We had also designed a kind of Rorschach test with pictures to be interpreted.

From the athletes' answers, on paper and orally, we could calculate their potential for aggressiveness, confidence, mental toughness, and control. We also added two different factors, an allowance for racial difference and a built-in lying factor, for those who thought they were smart enough to figure out the test and give the answers they thought we wanted.

Our Sports Dynamic Index was used by the New England Patriots and the Boston Celtics, but after about three years it was dropped because the athletes objected to it as unfair discrimination, and they were afraid that the material would be used against them if they were traded. One of the issues of the players' strike in 1973 was that they didn't want psychological testing.

The Penn hockey team tried the test because I was an alumnus, but did not apply it to their selections. At the end of the season their coach told me, "If I'd believed the test results at the beginning of the year, I'd have saved myself a lot of aggravation. The 'troublemaker' *was* the troublemaker. The 'leader' you identified did emerge as the leader."

Now I hear that the scouting process once again includes psychological testing, but this is twenty years later, so I guess we were ahead of our time.

We never made any money with the Sports Dynamic Index, but we got a lot of kudos, and I had a wonderful time meeting so many athletes who were my glamorous heroes. I have their signatures and messages to remember them by.

Jim Lonborg, who won the Cy Young Most Valuable Pitcher award, turned up to see us with a sore and swollen mouth after a tooth extraction. His wife had the car, so he came on a motorbike in a snowstorm, a tall, good-looking, articulate man who wrote on an autographed picture for me, "With your thoughts and influence, baseball can again be the number one sport in America."

After visiting me, All-Pro footballer Russ Francis wrote, "It was a real pleasure discussing with you what makes us tick. I'll come back for more, to find out, no doubt, that we are all only sophisticated neolithic cave dwellers after all."

Originally I wanted to make the Sports Dynamic Index the basis for my master's thesis in the field of experimental and clinical psychology, but it wasn't considered suitable because Brandeis was more involved in theoretical work. Dr. Maher had gone to Harvard and my new psychology professor Jim Lackner introduced me to psycholinguistics with a course titled "Language and the Mind." A few of the classes came to my house, and I used tapes and notes from other students and had a tutorial once or twice a month.

The theme emerged very soon. Instead of studying other people by interviews, observation, and maybe guesswork, I would study something much closer to hand—my own experience and discoveries in learning to adapt my speech to the rhythm of the rocking bed or the chest respirator and to the air that I was able to collect in my lungs through frog breathing. The title of my thesis was "Some Adaptive Compensations in Speech Control Achieved after Respiratory Paralysis—a Personal Case."

*   *   *

The children were growing up in the confusing times of Vietnam and the rebellious, liberated demands of the Sixties, which had not yet settled down into the more evenhanded values of the Seventies.

Susie was a butterfly in the Newton school system, out every evening and every weekend night. She was making a rather violent bid for independence, and neither Dottie nor I really knew how to deal with her. David was at Roxbury Latin School, preparing for college. It would have been fun to have been able to discuss their lives and my own new studies while we all had dinner together in my room.

The children were a captive audience for my views on psychology. I wanted to explore their developing minds and to hear serious and important things about their work at school. I asked them profound questions like, "What is your philosophy of life?" But they were only interested in gossip, what they heard in the corridor, who was hanging out with who on the corner by the store, feeble esoteric jokes, and a blanket condemnation of all teachers.

I had no patience to listen to junk. I was irritated with them when they slopped their drinks or used their forks the wrong way or ate with their dirty fingers. That would have shocked my meticulous Uncle Hy, who used to inspect my hands before each meal and send me away from the table to wash.

For two years, until Dottie started to serve the children in the dining room after feeding me, everyone had indigestion. The turmoil and frustration were as bad as in the old days when we used to eat in the kitchen, with Susie throwing food around from her high chair. We didn't seem to have progressed very far.

Freud was still my guiding light, and David was infuriated by my obsessive habit of analyzing everything. He had heard all he could take about Freud.

"Fraud! Fraud! Fraud!" he would yell and take his hands out of the food to put them over his ears.

Well, we had wanted our children to grow up as normally as possible, and now we had a normal teenage household, where the only thing the parents could be sure of was that everything they did was wrong.

We were lucky that David did nothing worse than eat with his fingers and yell at me.

David

He and I are still as close as when I was a child, and I think we're very alike.

As I grew up, he was just as accessible in his big new room at the end of the house. There was this man, always willing to talk. When I went to California to work on a film, I called home a lot, and he was always there, except once when he and Mom had gone out somewhere, and that really shook me. I'd got so used to the phone always being answered at my house, like a twenty-four-hour hotline. It made home seem very well rooted.

In her teens, my sister stopped talking to Dad for a bit, but I never did. We never lost touch or fought seriously, even when I was an adolescent. I didn't go through much of a rebellion, because I was still too worried about pleasing my parents, my mother because she could make your life hell if you didn't, and my father because he needed it.

My care of him increased in progressive stages. I was in Junior High School when I first helped him with the bedpan. How many kids handle their fathers that way? But it wasn't a big deal. He wanted the bedpan, he had to be helped, I was available, so I helped.

The first time I did it, he cried. Not because he was humiliated. They were tears of joy because he was so glad that I could do it for him so easily. It had been a barrier that a traditional upbringing made him feel was difficult to cross. But I didn't feel that way. He had to use the bedpan and Mom couldn't be there every minute.

Next to my mother, I know most about the whole situation, probably because I'm the oldest child. But there are things I still haven't done for Dad, because Mom doesn't give me a chance. She has to do it herself.

Even now, she'll be on the couch exhausted and I'm in a chair watching television. He needs his head moved to the right.

"Dottie!"

I jump up to do it, but he still asks for her, because she's been doing it all these years and she does it the best. She knows better than anybody what he needs, and he wants that comfort.

I've never gone through the whole process of putting him to bed at night. I've never put on the respirator belt for the wheelchair. My mother has never let me work the lifter. She knows that I should know how to do these things, but when she's there, she has to be doing everything all the time.

For example, the other night he wanted his pants changed before we all went out. I helped her to take off the pants. To put the others on him, she runs to one side and puts them on that leg, then runs to the other side of the bed, cuts in front of me, and starts pulling up on the other side.

That's a very simple operation I could be sure of doing right, but she doesn't give you a chance. She's got to do it because that's the way she is. No one else can do anything right. It's that same powerful confidence that has made her take care of my father so well all these years.

One reason she was always so busy, even when they started to get enough attendants, was because she thought she was the only one who could do it. So did Dad. When she goes out by herself, she's always late for everything, because he'll want something done at the last minute, and she'll do it, even if the attendant is around.

If she's not there, then it's me. If I'm visiting the house, he wants me, not the attendant. Things haven't changed

163

much since I was a child when it used to take me fifteen minutes to leave the house, but I figure, so what? It's my father. He needs me. If my arm itches, I can scratch it. He can't. I'm a fidgeter. I have to shift and move around all the time, and I can imagine what it must be like for him to feel fidgety and not be able to do anything about it.

As much as we have to do for him, there's a lot he doesn't ask for, just tries to live with. I have to remember that, for him, every day is a fight. He's always in pain. There is never no pain. It's just a question of what level of pain.

His friends still do a lot more for him than they would for anybody else, partly because of the way he is, partly because it's a sort of catharsis for them. Some of the very successful ones with very busy lives—one of the few people they take time out for is Dad.

"Here's my good thing I do. I go over to Lou's and spend the whole evening with him, even though I'm so incredibly busy."

That makes them feel good about themselves, and it's not difficult, because he's such good company and so adept at drawing people out and making them feel pleased and comfortable.

In California, I read about a man who'd been a quadriplegic for two years after an accident. His wife couldn't stick it. She wanted a divorce, and there was a custody battle, because he wanted the children and she said he couldn't possibly take care of them.

I called him at the hospital and said I was the son of a quadriplegic who had been quite capable of bringing up his children, and that we hadn't suffered in any way; and I offered to testify in court, if that would help.

But when I went to see him, I hated him. He was unpleasant to be with and had a really bad attitude, as if he thought the world owed him a living. I was glad I'd called him, but disturbed after I'd been to see him. I was never asked to testify.

I shouldn't think he has many of the helpful and loving friends my father has always had. When I was a child, I had this high ideal of what friendship was, but I grew up and found out that friends aren't like that all the time.

I expect more from friends, and I've tried to give more—sometimes way too much—and got burned as a result. I've learned to be more realistic, but I still expect much more from people than I get, and sometimes that hurts.

In California, there was none of the give and take I'd been used to with Dad and his business friends who wanted to be helpful. In Los Angeles, its the nature of the film business to engage in a lot of talk, lunches, meetings, etc., and most of the time, nothing happens. People rarely follow through on what they say. It was a crushing experience for me at first, the polar opposite of what I'd known at home in Boston, but it taught me how life worked.

When I left, it was hard for my parents, especially my mother, because she lost the security of me being there to take over when she was away. My father's attitude was, "If he goes to make movies in California, that shows that my illness isn't affecting his life, and that's what I want." My mother wanted that, too, but only in theory.

California is the best place for me to work, but I moved back to Boston for numerous reasons, one being what I saw as a deterioration in my parents' relationship. Mom would call to complain about Dad, while Dad would call to complain about Mom. I knew it was the years of sacrifice and stress taking their toll, and I felt that my presence might take some of the pressure off, and help them.

I'm the one Dad talks to in his down moments, but trying

to comfort him is like trying to comfort someone over a death in the family—there really isn't anything you can do about it. He's not going to get up and move tomorrow, and the pain isn't going to go away. I just try to help him to channel it into positive acceptance. He does the same for me. My being around helps, so moving back has been worthwhile.

As we go on, there will be more and more times when I'll need to be around.

As a child, it was all gains. The losses are now, and I see it as more of a sacrifice than I used to. At this point, I ought to be living my own life. I've made the break, yet my life is still partly ruled by the situation at home. It always will be. Any decision I make has ramifications most people don't have to face.

Sometimes I do battle, like the devil and God both pulling at me.

I say, "The heck with it, you've got to go and live your own life."

"Yes, but it's Dad. It's my parents. We love each other. If I don't do this or that good thing for them, then this or that bad thing will happen."

Where am I going to live? How will it affect my relationships? There will always be this pressure on my life, because if Mom should die first or get sick, I'd have to drop everything and come back here to take care of my father, at least until things stabilized and we figured out what to do.

There's always this knowledge at the back of my mind that it probably will fall on me. They don't want that, of course. My father says, "I'll live in a hospital," and I say, "The hell you will." It would be the worst thing that could happen to him. We might never be able to get him out again.

If they fight, Dad says, "OK, I'll get out of your way and

go live in a hospital," and Mom says, "There's the door. See if anyone will take you." Then they both call me.

But right now, if the right situation materialized in California, I'd go back.

Susie By the time I was in my teens, I'd stopped accepting the situation and thinking it was normal. It became the focus of my rebellion.

My father and I didn't get along at all. I was against the whole thing. It was too much. Every time I went in or out of the house, I was supposed to go in and give him a long explanation of where I was going or where I'd been and what was going on. When you're that age and your parents ask, "Where have you been?" or "Where are you going?" you can only say, "Out." You don't want to talk to them.

If my father and I had a fight, my mother would tell me, "Look, he can't come to you and make up. You have to go in there to him."

That killed me. I was very stubborn when I was fourteen or fifteen. I didn't get along with her either. I couldn't stand either of them, and they couldn't stand me.

But I grew up, and they grew up, and we've all changed. Now that I've broken away from my family, I can look back and love them as the people they are, without feeling obligations or guilt.

I should have . . . I shouldn't have. Look at them, I used to think. They're stuck there, and I can do what I want.

I don't feel that anymore, although I get a bit angry now, because I'm close to the age my mother was when it happened, and I have all this freedom, and she was tied down with two small children and Dad in that bed.

In high school and at college, I was more self-conscious about telling people what went on at home. I didn't tell new friends right away, because I've never liked to tell a whole lot of personal things too soon, and when I did eventually tell them about Dad, it was difficult to do, and I got very upset.

There were all kinds of pressures about dating. A casual date grew into a big deal. If a guy called for me, I couldn't just introduce him to my parents—"Hi, Mr. Sternburg. Hi, Mrs. Sternburg"—and go straight out. We'd have to hang around and talk, and it was all too much.

Some of my boyfriends couldn't believe it. It was hard to prepare them for what they were going to see, and they were really shocked.

To me, it's no big deal, but it has a terrific effect on some people. They can't believe that anyone can make such a commitment and give each other so much.

They come back, my friends do, even when I'm not there. They love my father, and if they're in Boston, they always want to see him.

He and I are very close now. We have wonderful talks, although I'm not physically close to him in the way David is, because I don't take care of him. I feed him and move his hands and legs, but he would never let me undress him or anything like that.

Because David can take care of Dad, he feels much more responsible than I do, and he feels in some way guilty. That's crazy, but it doesn't seem crazy to him, because that's the way he feels.

My father has always suffered from guilt, too. That's equally crazy, but if you feel it, you feel it. He used to tell me about that and dump his bad feelings onto me. My mother never dumped in the old days, but she does now. We talk about everything, because she knows that I won't think, "Oh my God, she's sick of it, she's going to walk out." She's just unloading.

She needs a break, but then so does he. They have to be apart once in a while, but nobody can look after him like she does. Nobody cares in the same way. She really loves him.

I find I expect more of people because I've grown up with two people who understand loving and giving, to each other and to everyone else. I get far more from them than they get from me. I hope my father realizes that, but he's so hard on himself—as if life hadn't been hard enough on him already.

The other day I was there, and he was very uncomfortable and in a lot of pain. It's difficult to watch, because there's nothing you can do. I left, and later I called. "Daddy, I got the feeling you really didn't want me around." And he said, "That's true, but I do now."

We don't spend a lot of time together these days, but I know he understands. I used to think I hurt him, but now we have such a strong bond that we're sure of how we feel about each other, and we don't have to keep proving it. If he needed me, he'd call, and I'd go at once.

My parents' main goal was always to bring us up as normal children, and they've succeeded. I don't necessarily think of them first. I wouldn't change my whole life for them. That was their aim for us, and they did a good job.

I'd go anywhere I wanted, but if Mom died, I'd come back, and wherever my father lived, whether he was in a hospital or not, it would have to be close to me.

It's difficult for David to make a decision about going back to California. He has a tougher time than I do, because he does more for Dad.

My parents say to me, "We don't ask you to help," and I say, "Fine, then don't." I used to feel bad about that, but I could spend every day doing something for them—there's so much to do—and I have a life and a career and dozens of other things, and if I don't break away from this, I'll never have my own life.

I haven't settled down and had a family, because my

experience has given me mixed feelings about having children, and I value my freedom. I resent the idea of waiting on a man. He and I would have to be absolutely equal, or I couldn't live with him. I don't want to make dinner every night.

Recently my brother and I sat down together for the first time and talked for hours about Dad and what would happen if my mother died.

David was talking about the burden of what he would have to do, and I said, "David! You're being totally unrealistic. They may want us to help and run errands, but they'd never want either of us to give up our lives." My father would never stand for it. I said, "David, you're crazy. It would put him in an awful position. He'd be uncomfortable every time I walked in the door. *I know him*."

I'm lucky he is like that. It takes a lot of intelligence to be the way he is, and emotionally, it must have been very tough, what he's managed to do with his life, what he's made of himself.

He's my favorite person in the world, he really is, and I admire him more than anyone. He looks for things to like in everyone, and he has a fantastic sense of humor. He must have been a lot of fun . . . I mean, he still is, but it's my great regret that we have never gone out together. We've never danced together.

thirteen

Poliomyelitis is an ancient disease. A skeleton of 3700 B.C. found in Egypt shows the effects of polio, and so does a 1300 B.C. carving of a crippled youth.

The disease was first identified and recorded in the late eighteenth century, and fifty years later it was widespread in Europe and India. Its name comes from the Greek word for "gray," *polios*, denoting the gray matter of the nervous system, and *myelos*, for the myelin sheath around certain nerve fibers.

At the beginning of this century, a Swedish doctor discovered that it is transmitted from person to person from the throat and intestinal tract. Paralysis develops because the virus kills motor nerve cells in the spinal cord that control various muscles. In some cases, healthy nerve cells sprout new connecting fibers to take over the work of the dead cells and the paralysis is only temporary, as I always thought mine would be. But I am one of the less than one percent of cases in which the paralysis is permanent.

Early epidemics in this country, usually in the summer, began to replace TB as a major childhood scourge. In the Northeast in 1916, 27,000 people, mostly children, were disabled, and 6,000 of them died. In the summer of 1921, polio struck Franklin Roosevelt, and the history of the disease began to change. He learned to walk again with crutches, and when he was president, he concealed his handicap by being seated during his public appearances. He founded the Georgia Warm

Springs Foundation for the care and therapy of polio patients and in 1938 the National Foundation for Infantile Paralysis, the March of Dimes, for research to conquer the disease.

While scientists searched for a vaccine, wave after wave of polio epidemics hit the United States and Europe in the warm weather, and summers became times of fear for many parents. Some children wore little packets of camphor around their necks, a useless folk remedy to ward off the disease. Some were sent away from the cities, and if the polio scare hit their town while they were away, they were quarantined, and if they ran even a low fever, the whole community was isolated.

Schools didn't open on time, people drank bottled water and kept their children away from the beaches or anywhere where there were crowds. Doctors would not do tonsillectomies, for fear of polio infection. In 1950, 35,000 people caught polio, and 3,000 of them suffered varying degrees of paralysis. Who would get it next? Adults were at risk now, as well as children.

The sixteen regional respiratory centers started by the March of Dimes saved many lives, thanks to the earlier development of the iron lung. Then in 1954, a forty-year-old researcher named Jonas Salk discovered that a healthy primate injected with a dead polio virus would develop immunity.

POLIO 90% BEATEN, stated a headline in *The Boston Globe* of April 12, 1955: END OF DREAD CRIPPLING DISEASE WITHIN SPACE OF 2 YEARS NOW SEEN A POSSIBILITY. Too late for me. Only three and a half months later I was stricken.

Later that year, millions of children and adults were innoculated with Dr. Salk's inactivated polio-virus vaccine, replaced four years later by Dr. Albert Sabin's live oral vaccine, which is used today.

The rehab centers closed, and by 1959 I was one of only twelve hundred polio survivors still on respirators. New cases decreased spectacularly, until there are now less than fifteen a year in the United States. But polio still claims millions of victims in tropical countries, especially where there is crowding and poor sanitation. Major fund-raising efforts, like the "We Are the World " recording by dozens of rock stars, bring vaccine to fight polio, as well as hunger.

The Salk and Sabin vaccines wiped out polio, and most young people, thank God, have no idea what it is, but there are 300,000 of us survivors with disabilities ranging from none to quadriplegia complicated by complete respiratory paralysis. An unexpected legacy is the appearance of new "post-polio symptoms." Twenty or thirty years after the illness, fatigue may develop, as well as pain in joints and muscles, increasing weakness, and sometimes atrophy, possibly because the nerve cells that took over from the dead ones are exhausted from years of doing an extra job. With me, they never did do that. My muscles were knocked out from the beginning, but I have developed osteoporosis and the risk of hidden fractures because the bones are soft. I also get tired more easily. I "hit the wall of fatigue," as runners say when they flag during a marathon, but like them, I can usually struggle through that and get my second wind.

Of the eight million handicapped people in this country, I have the dubious distinction of being one of the most severely disabled.

Thanks to organized efforts by other handicapped people, life is getting less difficult for us, with more conveniences like special parking places and ramps into many public buildings. At least people are becoming more aware of what we need, although most of them can't really imagine how we feel.

"When you sit in a wheelchair, you lose your height, and you become an it," Itzhak Perlman, the violinist, says. "You are your disability. I'm tired of being a human interest story, a brave handicapped musician. I'm a musician for whom life is not easy, but then is life easy for anyone?"

There are many things I dislike about my wheelchair: being lifted up and down stairs, the pain of sitting in it and feeling every pebble we go over because it has no shock absorbers, squeezing into small elevators, having to go on roundabout routes through kitchens and service corridors, going first into any public room, restaurant, or gathering. There I am, exposed. Maybe Dottie should put on a harness and pull me in, so that people will see her first.

My friends and family have learned how to treat me, of course. If we're having a party in my room, they come and sit on the high stools by the bed and talk to me for a while, as easily as they move away and talk to someone else at the other end of the room. They are so used to me rocking or wearing a respirator in a wheelchair that they see me, not the bed or the chair. But with people I don't know well, they see the chair with me in it, not just me.

When I'm out, I have the cruel illusion of being mobile, but I'm still stuck, because I can't go to people. I must wait for them to come to me. If Dottie and I go to a big formal lunch with many tables, ours is always the last table to be filled. The first person who risks it sits diametrically opposite me and either talks a lot or says nothing. Sometimes at a large party strangers come over immediately and make a big fuss over me, which is nice, but then I can see them wondering how they can get away.

When they avoid me, it's either because they don't trust themselves to know what to say or perhaps because I am an uncomfortable reminder that life is not always just and fair. I understood this better last year, when I went straight from watching a Boston Celtics practice to see my father-in-law in the hospital after an operation for cancer. The contrast between those powerful, healthy young athletes and the patients in the hospital, wracked and wasted, their life and energy standing still, was shocking and sobering. It explains why some people want to avoid me. I wonder if they realize that I notice.

Children and teenagers do better.

They accost me in a shopping mall. "What happened to you, mister? Why are you in that chair?"

"I got sick a long time ago."

The children wander off. The teenagers ask, "What from?"

"Polio."

"Huh? What's that?"

"Something you don't have to worry about."

"Yeah? Well . . . see ya."

Before I got polio, I had been as unaware of the working movements of my body as any of those children and teenagers, to whom I am an object of curiosity, not of pity.

My body was automatic. It just worked. I neither knew nor cared what happened with my brain and nerves and muscles when I hit a golf ball, jitterbugged on the dance floor, or smashed into a tennis serve. Everybody could talk and walk and run and breathe and make precise movements with their fingers. Like everyone else, I took those things for granted, until I lost them. One of the things I learned during the years of my late-blooming academic career at Brandeis was to marvel at the complex efficiency of simple movements, particularly of the totally unconscious physical mechanism of speech.

When you are going to speak, you decide what you want to say, often in a split second, although the exact words may be unknown to you until they come out. You speak them one after the other, but as they are articulated, each word has been fitted in with the ones preceding and following it. A short sentence only needs a small amount of air, and before you make a sound, your brain has already sent down the order for an appropriate breath. For a longer sentence, the brain adapts immediately and tells the lungs to take a deeper breath.

Ever since my lungs stopped working on their own, I haven't been able to do that. For example, in the hospital, I would want to speak, to call out, but there was no power in my voice. I was limited to the cycle of the iron lung. My sentences were short, and interrupted by the alternating phases of the machine. There was no unity between my brain, my tongue, and the breathing mechanism. Because my timing was off, I could only speak in short phrases and broken up syllables: "The Comm . . . on . . . wealth of Mass . . . achu . . . setts."

In a fairly short time, I had adapted subconsciously to my new environment and was matching my speech to the air made available by the machine. Since I have been on the rocking bed, I have adapted my speech to its rhythm in such a way that I speak sentences in whole unbroken clauses like anyone else. However, if you could stand by my bed and ask me a question, you might notice that I wait for the bed to give me enough breath before I answer.

If Dottie switches off the bed and puts on the chest respirator, I'll adapt to its different cycle without even knowing that I'm doing it, and if she turns off the respirator and I frog breathe, I can control the amount of air I collect and speak in longer sentences that are very close to normal.

Years after my lungs lost their power, my reading for the master's program included the experiments conducted in the 1960s by Donald Wilson at Stanford, which showed that sensory feedback can be used by the nervous system to enable the animal to adjust immediately to genetically unpredictable conditions of the body or environment without recourse to learning mechanisms.

"The locust has four wings. Recently I cut whole wings from several locusts, threw the locusts into the air and found to my surprise that they flew quite well. The flying locust shows ability to adapt to the loss. For the crippled locust to fly, it must change its motor output pattern."

For "fly" substitute "speak," and Wilson is talking about me. Biologically, that puts me on a par with the locust. When people ask me, "Where do you get the strength to fight back and carry on with your life?" I might answer, "Same place as the locust." I too have been able to change my motor output pattern to the point where very few people realize, especially on the phone, that I am not speaking in the same normal way that they are. Because the rocking bed and the chest respirator have a regular and predictable cycle, I can speak fluently. Human beings organize thoughts and then transform them into speech. Our brains are capable of racing far ahead of what we are saying, sometimes with unexpected results. Spoonerisms are an example: "Let me sew you to your sheet." The famous character who addressed Queen Victoria as "Queer Dean" had to have thought of the word "Queen" at the same time as he thought of the word "Dear," or it wouldn't have come out like that.

I never cease to marvel at the creativeness of human language, a window of communication that enables us to see how the mind works. Jim Lackner's course "Language and the Mind" dealt with Noam Chomsky's generative grammar theory, which shows that, without being taught, anyone can instinctively create a sentence that has never been heard before.

Jim was the first teacher who brought a class to me at home. I was tremendously excited. My classmates sat on chairs and on the floor while Jim lectured on the complexity and sophistication of the synchronization of exhaled breath with the mind and the face, jaw, and throat muscles. He went on and on. My eyelids began to close. I did everything I could to stay awake, shook my head, asked for a glass of water, rolled my eyes, looked at everything else in the room besides the speaker, and yet I dozed off. Not for more than a few seconds, but, boy, was I embarrassed. My first class in twenty-five years, and I fell asleep. I woke abruptly and looked at Jim.

He either had not noticed or pretended not to. To stay awake, I began to ask questions like crazy. Pretty soon, Jim and I were having a discussion, while the other students slept.

A few more classes came to my house, but mostly I read books by people like Karl Lashley and Charles Sherrington and listened to tapes of lectures and discussions. Although I got very tired and dropped back into depression and frustration from time to time, it was a wonderful discovery to find that I could make up for my useless body by living a stimulating and active life of the mind.

My increasing openness to new ideas led me to explore other things that would be helpful, and I took a course in Transcendental Meditation in the hope of lowering my blood pressure and becoming more tranquil and better able to understand myself.

David's college roommate Bill was very involved in meditation. He would sit in my room and meditate while we were waiting for Dottie to bring in the dinner, and he said that it worked for him. He could do it anywhere, so I thought, if he can do it on the subway or a rattling trolley car or while David and I are listening to jazz, why can't I do it on my rocking bed?

Dottie took the course with me. We couldn't go to a group, so a guru came to us wearing space shoes and bringing a picture of the Maharishi, and we learned the simple techniques and went through the ceremony with the flowers and fruit and the white handkerchief to be given our mantras.

I was torn two ways. I wanted the peace of meditation, and yet I fought against it. Trying to control the turmoil of thoughts that prevented my mind from reaching the deeper level of consciousness was like trying to domesticate a wild animal. The guru persevered gently, and I finally reached the point of resignation where I could allow my thoughts to rise like bubbles from the ocean floor and let them go without hanging onto them and wrestling with them or pursuing them into their labyrinths.

After her first enthusiasm, Dottie dropped out fairly soon, because she couldn't spare time for the twenty minutes morning and evening. I meditated faithfully for two years before I began to slacken off. I always found it difficult, but it did relax me and lower my blood pressure, and it gave me an insight into thought processes and improved my concentration, so that I worked better.

I became more contemplative and began to explore some different religions. Meditation stimulated my interest in Buddhism, and I was enticed by the Noble Truths, which start with the concept that desire and the entrapment of time create unhappiness, suffering, and despair. Letting go of desire brings peace of mind. I longed for that, but I wasn't ready to abandon desire and the pursuit of earthly happiness.

Confucius tells me that "Human fulfillment does not come simply by means of association with other people, but arises as the result of the faithful relation between the individual and the transcendent God."

Jesus said from a hilltop, "Take no thought for your life, what you shall eat or what you shall drink; nor yet for your body, what you shall put on. Is not the life more than meat, and the body than raiment?"

I wanted to take a middle road. I felt that I was justified by the words of William James: "Who can decide offhand which is absolutely better: to live, or to understand life? We must do both alternately, and a man can no more limit himself to either, than a pair of scissors can cut with a single one of its blades."

After reading *Totem and Taboo*, I was still entranced by Freud's theory that religion stems from trauma-induced neurotic symptoms and is man-made from a sublimated sexual drive. The superego, or conscience, evolved into rules and laws that governed early civilizations and eventually organized religion. I did believe in a speculative way in a Supreme Being beyond my reach, but I had no faith that any formal religion could bring me closer to God.

It was at this time that a new attendant came into my life, bearing another gift, the most valuable of all.

My initial pleasure at the new experience of being able to be submerged and washed in a real bathtub was beginning to wear off. Everything had gone all right so far, but because of my underlying fear of death, I was still waiting for that other shoe to drop. Why shouldn't the next trip to the tub be my last?

Although my other dominating fear, of losing Dottie, had not prevented me from allowing her more freedom for a life of her own, I was still struggling with the fear of abandonment. She was out of the house more, and I was lonelier. Using the tub bath kept her with me for an extra half-day, but using the tub was a terrifying ordeal, led up to by hours of anxiety and dread.

Balancing my fears, it seemed that the fear of death was the stronger, so I sometimes cut down the baths to less than two a week. I should have known from past experience that not facing fear won't conquer it, but emotion can blot out the useful lessons of history and leave you with the ruinous ones, like my devastating terror in the old Hubbard tub at the rehab center.

I was ready for someone like Mike.

Michael Mastrosimone answered our advertisement for a "concerned person." He was an Italian, short but very strong and muscular, with dark skin and thick black hair. His family sold vegetables in the street market, and he was setting up programs for disadvantaged children and needed a daytime job. He was a Roman Catholic whose own struggles with life had left him with deep feelings for his fellow man and an unshakable faith in God.

Before every bath morning, I was awake half the night and couldn't eat breakfast or do anything but lie helplessly engulfed in my own terror.

Up in the lifter, past the bookshelves in my room, over the small bump between wood and tile, past the sunny window, and—oh, my God, the moment of terror—down into the tub. As the water crept over me, my frog breathing became labored, and I usually panicked and pleaded with Dottie to take me out at once. My head was pounding, it was going to blow up.

While I screamed to get out, Dottie kept up a running flow of talk while she washed me, and Mike called out encouragement from the other room where he was making up the bed.

When I was finally back there, swaddled in towels, I felt clean and fresh but absolutely exhausted, not from the ordeal but from my own terror of it.

One morning when Dottie had left Mike to finish dressing me, I admitted to him, "I wish we'd never had the tub put in. I know it's safe, but—" I frog breathed enough air to say it—"I know that one day it will kill me."

"Not likely." Mike shook his head.

"My mind knows that, but my fear doesn't. What am I going to do?"

"Try faith," Mike said. "Open the window of faith and let yourself trust in a Supreme Being to protect you. I don't care what you do or how you do it. Just try."

I didn't say anymore, but the next time I was rolled into the bathroom, tense with panic and ready to scream at Dottie to stop before she had even begun, the sunlight from the window passed over my face. With a great effort of my mind, I pushed open that other window, and the light poured in with the confirmation of all the unrealized longings and beliefs. And I knew that I was not alone.

"Better that time," Dottie said fifteen minutes later, as she and Mike settled me back into bed.

"You open the window?" Mike looked at me with his dark, thoughtful eyes.

"No, it's too cold," Dottie said, but I nodded.

The fear of the tub did not go away, but I learned how to overcome the fear, as a spiritual dimension crept into my life, and the Supreme Being came closer into focus. The trips to the tub reinforced my new assurance that I did have weapons against fear. Hanging helplessly in the canvas sling, I knew that, with God, I was not alone. As Mike and I explored avenues of prayer that led to peace, I passed beyond the Freudian doubt and limitations to understand that faith and psychology can live together without conflict and that, within them both, we make our own choices.

My growing belief gradually returned me to the faith in myself that I thought I had lost forever when I lost movement and breathing. Mike taught me to trust God with my life, which didn't take away my own responsibility and confidence, but rather increased it.

Through the window that Mike had helped me to open, I looked for answers to the question I had been asking for years. Why me? In my search among different religious beliefs, psychology, philosophy, and metaphysics, I came to the Old Testament and found myself particularly at home with the Book of Job.

Dottie had taken a course on the Book of Job at Smith. She took me to one of the lectures, and we discussed it at some length at home, but it wasn't until I had experienced my own ordeal of pain and loss that I began to see the message clearly.

Job lost everything, health, children, possessions. Like me, he experienced a suffering that could not be understood. After several readings, I gradually came to see that goodness and evil have nothing to do with the reason for suffering. Because the reason is not yet apparent to us, many people choose to call it random chance. I choose to believe that there is a rational explanation, and although it has not yet been revealed, I find comfort in my belief that there is a reason for my suffering. Because Mike started me on the road to faith, I was able to stop wasting energy asking, "Why me? Why has this happened to me?" and say more productively, "I don't know why this happened, but I know where I get the strength to cope with it."

The outcome of my search for enlightenment was a renewal of my Jewish faith, or rather a discovery, since I had never given it much thought. My grandparents came from Poland and Russia, and as a baby, I spoke with a thick Yiddish accent. My parents' generation of Jewish immigrant families was less interested in religion than in becoming assimilated here. Our goal was to be completely Americanized.

My parents observed the formal requirements of Judaism but not much more. You sent your son to Hebrew school, and after his Bar Mitzvah he was a full member of the congregation, and you didn't need to worry anymore about his soul. Dottie had had even less instruction as a child. Her family went to temple on the High Holidays, and that was about all she knew.

All the time I was in Mass. General in the iron lung, no rabbi ever came near me, but a Catholic priest stopped by to see me every day and even brought me a radio so that I could listen to the Yom Kippur services that September. Those services had not moved me when I was free to take part in them, but then they made me cry.

Early every Sunday morning in the rehab center in Wellesley, there was either a Catholic or Protestant service. While I waited for breakfast, I listened to the words of faith and comfort and envied my Christian ward mates. A rabbi did come once to visit me there. He brought me a book about

183

Beethoven, but he was cold and distant, and I couldn't discuss anything that mattered with him. After some awkward small talk, he left and never came back.

Soon after I came home, a new young rabbi, Richard Yellin, took over my temple. He was enthusiastic and intelligent, and we formed an immediate bond and have been friends ever since. We saw each other often and talked about everything—politics, books, the history of mysticism, psychology—and he helped me to change my ideas about my Jewish inheritance.

Through Richard I began to understand my own religion and its potential for me. He laid the groundwork for my later decision that of all the beliefs I had studied, Judaism, with its respect for the dignity of all men and its basic Socratic command, "Know thyself, then extend thyself to reach out to others," was the most rational one for me.

My faith was tested when Dottie had to have a serious operation, and I had to rely on nurses and attendants for several weeks.

Dottie I had kept away from doctors as much as possible. Lou had enough for both of us, and I figured that, since they saw me in the house, they would notice if anything was wrong. But when I began to have female problems, I made an appointment for a checkup.

"There's a fibroid tumor I'll have to remove," the doctor told me.

"Can you do it now?" It didn't sound like anything serious.

"You'll have to make arrangements for a major operation. You'll be in the hospital eight to ten days and then recover at home for a couple of weeks."

My first thought was Lou. What would he do? This would be longer than any of my vacations, and I wouldn't be able to come home if there was a crisis. He was really starting to get his life together, and I didn't want another setback, but my own life was beginning to stall. David was in college and Susie about to go. I didn't have the empty nest syndrome, because my nest would never be empty with Lou there. Yet I was at that stage in my life when I had done my mothering, and now it was time to think of myself. My second thought was that I could have complete privacy and rest for at least a week, so I didn't dread the operation. I looked forward to it.

Our help situation was always in a state of flux, and that Thanksgiving we had a fairly new attendant who was not the most reliable. Maybe Lou should go to the hospital. But he wasn't going out anywhere, and how would he get home after my operation, and who would care for him then? A Swiss boy was living in and helping in the evenings. He was quite capable, and I would find more attendants and some nurses to be in charge.

Lou was stunned when I told him. Then his survival instinct took over, and he began to plan. We picked a date just before Christmas, when David would be home from college and Susie would be on vacation from school. Through friends, we found two nurses who came to me for two days' training before I left. Milt, Al Clark, Shelly, and Hank were all nearby at home and on call that week, and I spent an evening showing them how to make Lou comfortable and what to do in an emergency. Teams of friends were in reserve for shopping, visiting, any little jobs. Everyone wanted to help, and they brought me presents—nightgowns, perfume, books—for the hospital. I began to look forward to my rest.

If you ever have to have an operation, don't go to a hospital in Christmas week and expect to find it fully staffed. The nurses who are still there unwillingly are at Christmas parties when you need them. The care ranges from very little to none. If you can possibly afford it, have private nurses after major surgery, whatever anyone tells you. My luxurious week in bed turned out to be a nightmare of pain, neglect, and the solitude of not having a husband to help me through it. I wasn't as independent as I thought. When Lou was in the hospital, I had screamed, fought, pleaded, cajoled to get him proper attention. My friend Evie screamed at the staff for me but they didn't care. I couldn't wait to go home.

David and Susie, who had been wonderful to me, picked me up on Christmas day. I spent three hours dressing and putting on makeup, so Lou wouldn't know how weak I was. I could hardly pick up my comb, it was so heavy. I couldn't even stand up straight. When I crept into his room and he saw this little (I lost twelve pounds), gray-haired, hunched, shuffling remnant of his wife, I thought he was going to faint. He looked as ghastly as I did. I had not been ill for eighteen years, and he wasn't prepared for this, because he hadn't seen me in the hospital. He had thought I would come home ready to go to work again, and I could see on his face the lost thought, "Who's going to take care of me?"

My week alone had taught me a lot. I had somehow survived the hospital without decent nursing or the help of a husband, and I knew that this was the way it was going to be all my life. I had worked hard to make my children independent. Lou's parents and mine were getting old. Our friends were supportive, but they all had families and lives of their own. I was always going to have to count on myself.

Everyone came to see me when I was first home. They divided their attention between Lou and me, but as I got better, I faded into the background again. I was in my mid-forties and wondering how much longer I could cope with the constant everyday pressures and responsibilities. It would be hard to change my superwoman habits, but when my doctor found out how much physical work I'd been doing for Lou, he ordered no lifting or pulling for at least eight weeks. If I was going to change my routine, now was the time.

The nurses knew that I had been feeding Lou three meals a day and was perpetually on call for everything else. We hired a new orderly, and the nurses trained him to do everything, since they knew that Lou wouldn't want me to do that. I went back to work on different terms, and gradually Lou realized that, instead of loving him less, I would love him more if I had more freedom. This was my new beginning.

At first, he resented the idea that I wasn't going to be the only one to do all the things that made him more comfortable, and it was often difficult and painful for me to watch someone else struggling with things like putting on his shirt and perhaps hurting him in the process. I had to nail myself to the chair, so that I wouldn't jump up and do it myself and get it over with. Lou played tricks. He would ask me to take care of him all one day, because he was in pain or tired of the attendants, and I had to decide whether he was conning me or really needed me. I wanted always to be there when I was needed, but I didn't want to slip backward to the state I had been in when he first came home, when I was afraid to leave the house for fear he would die while I was out.

I had to tell myself that I was doing the best I could, although there were days when it hurt me to let the attendants take over. The women's movement was on my side in my struggle for more freedom, and Lou has realized now that what is often difficult for him is worth it, because it makes it easier for me.

We love each other even more now, and our marriage is closer.

fourteen

Sometimes when I can't sleep or when I've nothing better to do, I repeat to myself the names of all the people who have been with me in this strange, intimate relationship of strong young attendants and a man whose body is inferior and dependent on them but whose mind is free and equal.

Bob Park, Bob Doucette, Bob who played chess with me, Bob who left to be a truck driver. Audie from Nassau, Alvaro from Colombia, Jon from Beacon Hill. Charlie Ruddy, Byron, Vance, Hisashi, Wayne Soini, Zhou Yuan, and Manny Manasha from Iran.

George, Chet, Sam, Steve, Joe Drapala, Jim Fay, who was a flower child of the Sixties, Steve Potter, who was a flower child, too, the despair of his family, though not of ours.

Martha Cuzzi, Mary, Jan who sneaked off in the middle of the night, Patsy Bustos, and Merry, who wasn't. Paul Rabineau from Switzerland, Mike, Bill, Craig, Bruce, and Bruce Packey who was a minister of the Assembly of God. George Zabriski, Joe, Mitch, A. J. Brown, Jr., Larry McGinty, Philip, Wayne, Joe Pacheco, Jay, John, Gerry, Boyd, Dan Healy, Harry Flamm, Terrence O'Neil Joyce from New Zealand, Mike Mastrosimone from New Jersey.

My worldwide litany of friends and helpers, the players who have moved with me through the long drama and comedy of my illness.

Most of my attendants have been students between the ages of twenty-five and thirty-five, and they keep me stuck in time between those ages, so that I hope never to settle into middle age.

They fit their working hours here into their class schedules, and they bring a part of their life in with them. They are a window through which I can see what's going on out there in the world and keep up with changes in thought, values, trends, art, books, and music. Through them, I learned about modern jazz, the Beatles, the Rolling Stones, the hippies, the yippies, the anti-war and anti-nuclear movements, environmental protection and the works of the great thinkers of history, Freud, Gandhi, Mohammed, Buddha.

With them and my children, I traveled through pop songs, beat music, rock and roll, Bob Dylan and the protest folk songs, *Jesus Christ Superstar*, *Hair*, and soul. Mitch, a six-foot-six basketball player, taught me a lot about classical music and jazz. Hisashi, who came from an impressive Tokyo family background, opened the door for me to Oriental culture.

Steve was the first of the "protest" attendants, and there were quite a few, since the quiet humanity of doing this kind of job appeals to disenchanted young men who have dropped out of the conventional scene. Steve came to us looking like the Fifties, and I watched him become a Sixties hippie before my eyes, with strange, rebellious clothes and growing hair. His was the first long hair on a man Susie and David, who were eight and ten, had ever seen. Later, when they went through their own hippie phases, I saw Steve Potter recreated.

If I had lived out my life as a healthy suburban businessman and golfer, I would have been mostly among people of my own age, and I don't suppose I would have had much to do with the young as the years went on. As it is, young people are in and out of this house all the time, and they have opened me up to all kinds of new thoughts, as we share our interests and ideas. Even though my children are grown up and living independently, I still enjoy a continuous cavalcade of youth, which quite simply makes my life more bearable.

In 1975, I was fifty years old, and Dottie declared it to be "The Year of the Lou."

She remembered that when my Uncle Hy was fifty, he sent out an announcement to all his friends and asked them to say when they wanted to invite him for lunch, dinner, drinks, or a weekend.

He had a lot of friends and was as popular a guest as he was a host because he was clever and witty and well-read, with great style and charm and a fund of jokes, which made him the center of attention wherever he went. He was everybody's Uncle Hy, and he had a lovely fiftieth birthday, letting them celebrate him.

Dottie thought this was a great idea, to spread out the pleasure rather than concentrate it in just one party, and since I wasn't able to go out, her announcement asked everyone to say when they would come to my house, bringing something special.

During the Year of the Lou, some people brought a whole dinner, and some brought new friends I hadn't met. A.J., my young attendant, brought a jazz band. Harold Turin brought Michael Dukakis, the governor of Massachusetts. Some people brought musicians, a chamber group or a cello soloist. My friends Cynthia and David brought a small theater group to perform in my room a medley of poetry and comedy and dramatic speeches and some scenes from Shakespeare. It was the first live theater I had seen since I got sick, and it stimulated me to wild excitement.

My friend Sonny brought all his office staff, and Shelly Appel, whose company we represented, brought his entire work force of twenty-five people, with dinner for everyone.

The voices I had got to know so well on the end of the telephone became faces and friends.

I continued to study and dictate for my master's degree, and in 1978 I graduated after eight years of work. I couldn't go to Brandeis, so Brandeis came to me in caps and gowns—President Bernstein, Jim Lackner, Dean Lester Loomis, Dr. Brendan Maher, the lovable gray-haired Welshman with his old tweed suit under his gown, Hank Foster, who was on the board of trustees. They walked through the front garden and down the hall to my room, where I rocked away in a bright blue shirt, while they gave me my diploma, and my friends and family beamed and clapped. I have it all on video tape, because a television station sent cameras and a charming interviewer, and they filmed the whole thing.

When President Bernstein read the presentation and handed the diploma to David for me, I made a short speech, in which I said that I had started my academic venture—or adventure—with a purely selfish motive: "To try to understand human behavior and therefore my own personality, so that I could cope better with a unique condition. Even better, what I got out of it was support and enthusiasm, which strengthens my belief in human kindness and goodness. The combined efforts of everyone here has made this day possible . . ."

I told them that everyone shared in the honor, "which I consider to be a tribute to the perseverance of the human spirit," and then they all cheered and went out to the porch for a drink. We had a wonderful party and watched ourselves on the evening news.

The full television feature appeared later that year in a magazine program that was shown all over the country. I almost didn't watch it, because it conflicted with a Red Sox–Yankee game, but my ego conquered my devotion to baseball. A lot of other people watched it, too. I got letters from everywhere, even long afterwards, and when I started to go out again, somebody would always come over to me and say, "I saw you on television!"

The master's degree had seemed like the pinnacle of achievement. I thought it would be enough, but it wasn't very long before my restless spirit was asking, what now? What next? How do we top that?

After the ceremony in my room, Jim Lackner had said to me casually, "How about going on to a Ph.D., Lou?"

"That's crazy," I told him. "Way beyond me." But during the summer, I began to think about it. Instead of satisfying me, my success had made me hungry for more, and eventually I decided to start working for the doctorate in the fall, as long as it wouldn't jeopardize my business or health and as long as Jim Lackner could be my advisor.

By 1980 I had been on my rocking bed for twenty-four years. That was 126 million rocks and 94,000 miles that my bed and I had traveled through space, or roughly four times around the world. My mind had reached out to adventure, but where was my body going? All those painful miles had taken me nowhere. I was a man on a treadmill.

The television show had used clips from Uncle Hy's old home movies: me on the high school football team, me as a very young man kidding around in the garden, throwing a ball, swinging a baseball bat, walking joyfully to my car with Dottie the day we got engaged, holding my first baby in the sunlight—aching reminders of all those lovely times outdoors. When I saw on the screen the procession of gowned academics walking down my street under the trees and up the garden path through the lawn, I yearned for the lush summer greenness out there and all the life of the world that I was missing.

Where were we going, my friend and jailer, the rocking bed and me?

And then Aunt Fay came up from New York to visit. Aunt Fay was not a real aunt, but she had been Dottie's mother's best friend since they worked together in an office when they were both fourteen. Aunt Fay was a Greek lady, very close to her family and the families of her friends, but a completely emancipated woman, far ahead of her time. With a strong, large-featured face and a voice like a man, she had never married but had a good office job and went abroad by herself and drove a car and wore slacks in the early Thirties, long before women did things like that. Many years ago, she contracted muscular dystrophy, and she gradually became weaker and weaker. Eventually, Dottie's mother had gone to New York to say good-bye to Aunt Fay, who was barely alive. Dottie's mother herself died soon after that, and we thought that Aunt Fay must have died, too.

Until one day Dottie got a call. "Know who this is?"

"Well, I . . . I know your voice . . ." Dottie tried to fit a face to what she thought was a man's voice.

"It's Aunt Fay. I'm in Boston."

Incredibly, she had survived. In Goldwater Hospital in New York, she met a man named George who was paralyzed from polio and wore a chest respirator. The two of them had been on a ten-day trip in a van with a nurse and an attendant, staying in motels in Montreal and other places.

"George has a sister in Newton, so I'll come and see you and Louis and your Dad," she told Dottie.

"When?"

"This afternoon. You got any Southern Comfort?"

The van drove up. The attendant got out and let down a ramp at the back, and out rolled Aunt Fay in a motorized chair with her twisted fingers on a joy stick and a bumper sticker on the back of the chair that demanded SAVE GOLD-WATER HOSPITAL!

She rolled into my room, asking, "Where's my drink?" and

settled herself by my bed to tell me all about her trip. She had a permanent tracheotomy, with the tube attached to the hose of her respirator.

"Enough about me," she said after a while. "Where have you been lately, young Louis?"

"Here in bed. I don't go out."

"What do you mean, you don't go out?" She was shocked. "You've got to go out."

"Well . . . I've been thinking a bit more about it. Maybe one day I will."

"What do you mean, one day? Look at me. Look at George. He had polio, too. Get yourself out of here, you lazy bum. You've got it too damn easy. Get with it. Get back into the world."

After she and George went back to New York, Aunt Fay would call me almost every day. "You been out yet? When are you going out?"

Then she moved into a home where old and handicapped people lived independently. David went to see her every time he was in New York, and she continued to hound me, "When are you going out?"

Phil Marcus, a friend I had made on the phone through business, told us about a friend of his who had a fleet of ambulances that took handicapped people around during the week. They just sat in the garage at weekends, and Phil could borrow one if he liked, so that I could go out for a ride.

I had not been away from the house for fifteen years, since that last abortive attempt to go to a party, when I had made Dottie turn back. I was terrified, then excited and eager, then scared again. The ambulance would be very different from our old van. Dottie would drive, but could she handle it? What if she misjudged its size and bumped a curb? Would my chair tip over? Would I panic? What if we had an accident?

194

I had been safe at home, what the hell was I getting myself into?

The night of June 6, 1980, I managed to sleep at last and woke early, working myself up to a fever of excitement. Nothing could stop me now.

Except the rain. On Saturday, June 7, it poured all day, and I had to live through a whole interminable week before we finally took our first short trip.

With Dottie and Phil Marcus and A.J., I went to my friend Phil Jackson's house two streets away. I stayed in the ambulance and the Jacksons rushed out to welcome me in the driveway, as excited as if I were the Second Coming.

"Promise to take me home in ten minutes," I asked Dottie, but we were all talking and laughing, and I was so wound up that when Dottie backed the ambulance out to the street, I said, "Let's go by Harold Karlin's house and surprise him."

"I thought you wanted to go home."

"Not yet. Who else is near? Let's go on to Lois and Hank's place, too."

My ten-minute trip lasted a triumphant hour. I was energized by my friends' excitement and by Dr. Karlin's amazement and joy. Dottie drove carefully home at fifteen miles an hour, but I hadn't moved for so long that I kept telling her she would be stopped for speeding. At home, I floated six inches above the bed. I was so proud of myself. I had done it. It was over, and I had loved it.

When Phil left with Dottie to take the ambulance back, I asked him, "When do we go again?" If I didn't go out again soon, I might lose my nerve, as I had with the bathtub.

When Phil said, "Maybe I can ask my friend again in September," I was crushed. September, that was the end of time. I couldn't wait until then.

Dr. Karlin spoke to someone he knew in the ambulance business in Malden, and we were able to borrow a big van every Saturday. It was designed to take six chairs with their wheels fitting into slots in the floor. They sandbagged me into place. Dottie drove and A.J. sat in the back with me and an extra motor and hose and chest piece, in case.

At last, a real view of the world again, instead of edited versions of it from other people and unreal versions from television. The world had changed! I had never seen a McDonald's. The big sober cars I knew had become speeding and brightly colored and so small that I couldn't imagine how large men got into them. No hats on women, short skirts, bottoms moulded in tight jeans, braless bosoms bounding.

Boston was a new city. I saw for the first time the Prudential Tower, and the John Hancock glass skyscraper amazed me. Dear old Scollay Square, where twenty-five years ago I had staggered into my father's office because I was too ill to drive to any more customers, had disappeared under the stark and functional buildings of Government Center.

I had never seen an enclosed shopping mall. I went wild buying things for myself. I made Dottie wheel me into an expensive women's store and told her, "Buy what you like." My heart swelled with pride, because I could do something for her that I had loved to do as a young man.

We had such good times that soon we were asking ourselves, "Why only on Saturdays?" So we found a brown Ford van, which had been newly converted for a wheelchair and had everything we wanted: enough room for my chair, comfortable bucket seats in front, a hydraulic ramp, a low enough roof for any parking garage, even cruise control for when we went out on the highway for the long journeys we planned. Dottie took me for a ride around the block, and we bought it.

I went to the temple for Yom Kippur, and two thousand people in the congregation knew I was in circulation again. We went everywhere. Aunt Fay was proud of me. David was in Hollywood working on a film, and I had the crazy idea that, if I kept going, some day when he was a famous movie producer, I would fly out to California to see him get his Oscar.

Our short trips stretched into all-day adventures. I was willing to take risks. Although I was still afraid of the unknown, I found I could reach out for it, catch it, and make it familiar, then on to a new unknown, a new risk to tame.

Because I knew people from the sports world from the days of the Sports Dynamics Index, Bob Woolf, agent for the great Larry Bird, got me into Boston Celtics basketball practices. General Manager Red Auerbach had come to my house for a March of Dimes film, and he greeted me with "You're just as ugly as ever."

"Why don't you play me?" I asked.

"We would, but you can't go to your left." I loved the casual, joking acceptance.

My heroes all got to know me, and the players would come over and chat and joke, pretend to throw a ball at me— "Catch!"—and include me in everything that was going on.

We started going to the movies, which I have always loved. We still do that a lot. I sit at the top of the aisle, and I like the feeling of being with people without having to socialize if I don't want to. I'm with Dottie, perhaps David, or one of the attendants, but I'm alone, and everyone is quiet around me.

Hank and the curator of the Museum of Fine Arts took me to an exhibit of Anthony Caro's huge metal sculptures outside the Christian Science Center. I was intrigued by the great modern forms, and I wrote to Caro in England, and we began a long correspondence. I was very involved with my doctorate and thinking about language, and I told him that I thought the creation of a sentence was like sculpture. "You take words like blocks and put them in the order you want. Steel is your vocabulary."

The greatest thrill of all for me in that time of new liberation was going to rehearsals of the Boston Symphony Orchestra. Some of the musicians were Harold Karlin's patients, and he took me to Symphony Hall. The first time we went, Dottie

197

hit my toe against a wall as she turned the chair off the van ramp, and the freight elevator they use for pianos got stuck with me in it. As they parked me in a doorway of the balcony, frightened and shaky from the elevator, in agony from my toe, the orchestra began to play Beethoven's Fifth, and I was instantly in heaven.

When I was very young, Uncle Hy had started me off on music by taking me to rehearsals of the radio orchestra he conducted. I had first been exposed to Beethoven at ten when Estelle took me to a concert, and I was stunned by the Fifth Symphony. Now, because I had only been listening to records and tapes for years, I was overwhelmed by the quality and beauty of the sound. With the opening notes, my heart leaped up in ecstasy. Da da da *da*, the victory notes from World War II, my own little victory—I sat there and cried.

I went to Symphony Hall many times. Dottie got a cold, and I froze, because they keep the air conditioning very cold since the musicians work up a sweat when they are playing. I sat shivering under sweaters and blankets, and Seije Ozawa came up to give me an autographed picture after rehearsal. He was in his white jump suit and sneakers, with his hair all over the place from the athletic exertion of conducting a hundred artists in the music that exhilarated me.

The more I went out in the van, the less nervous I should have been, but I was still scared a lot of the time, and I still am, although we go out several times a week and sometimes more than once a day. In spite of all evidence to the contrary, this is still a risk. I've been lucky with it hundreds of times, but sooner or later, something is going to happen. And maybe now, this trip, this is going to be *it*. Shall I tell Dottie I don't want to go?

One of the ambitions that kept up my courage about going out was that I was looking ahead to the time when I would finish the work for my Ph.D. If I actually got it, I wanted to be at Brandeis on graduation day to receive it.

It took me four years to finish my thesis, and it involved more reading and writing and sheer concentrated thought than I would ever have thought I could manage.

Jim Lackner brought students to my room, and we had many seminars here. The students loved it, because it was very informal and productive and Dottie, of course, fed them. It was a great thrill for me, little old Louis Sternburg who had to repeat second grade because he couldn't do the work, to be living with so much intellectual stimulation. It made me impatient with social small talk, the same impatience I used to feel with David and Susie's school chatter at those disastrous family dinners. I can't do small talk anymore. It's no loss.

The work I was doing was an expansion and confirmation of my master's thesis. For that, I had been my own little lab in which I could study myself. I enlarged that now to include three other polio patients: Dick Higgins, who had been at the rehab center with me; Muriel Chiten, who was an iron lung patient with me at Mass. General; and Lily Manning, whom I had been told about by the respirator repair man, who loved and admired her.

Lily's husband was a doctor, and she lived with him in a house on the grounds of the hospital where he worked. Muriel was living in a hospital, and so was Dick. I was shocked when I went to see him at the hospital in Worcester. I remembered him as an elongated teenager on an oversize rocking bed, keeping the ward going with his jokes and good spirits. Now he seemed like an old man, gray and dwindled, his long body hunched in a chair. After doing much better than me at first, he had relapsed, and although he could still use a few back muscles to shift himself in the chair, it upset me to find that he seemed to have lost his fight and his enthusiasm for life.

He was breathing with a motor attached to his trachea, because of hypoxia, which meant he suffered a shortage of oxygen to the brain, a post-polio symptom that occurs as the lungs deteriorate. I have this sometimes, especially when waking in the morning. I feel dizzy, irritable, and confused and still as tired as if I hadn't slept. Now I have a machine that operates at night to filter out carbon dioxide and nitrogen so that I get more oxygen.

From tests done on my three subjects by Jim Lackner and some of his graduate students, and from my own questions and observation, I found that they had all adapted to artificial breathing and could produce normal speech, although they used shorter phrases than me and longer pauses. Like me, they had instinctively learned to fit the speech to the air available instead of the other way around. We discovered that we carried thoughts longer and spoke quite fast, since we wanted to get as many words as possible into the available breath. We found our timing was remarkably good because, although our motor nerves had been destroyed, the sensory nerves told us by touch and pressure exactly where the respirators were in their cycle.

We all read aloud excerpts from *Doctor Zhivago* and found it more difficult than free speech, because we were using Pasternak's phrases and sentences, not the ones we planned ourselves. With practice, we improved and were able to manage better expression and emphasis. When you have all the breath you want, you emphasize a word or syllable by giving it more air power. When you can't do that, you emphasize by speaking the preceding syllable comparatively softer, then delaying a fraction of a second or changing the pitch.

On May 6, 1982, I was to make the oral defense of my dissertation to a committee of three professors and other academics and graduate students who would come with them. I was going to have to explain why I had done the experiments, how I did them, and what the results were. I think I was more frightened of this exam than of any physical torture I had ever had to go through as a patient. Three weeks before, Dottie and I went to Jim and Ann Lackner's house in the country to sit in the sun and discuss how I should plan my defense and to review the main points I had been dealing with in the twelve years since I began working for my master's.

At home, Dottie and I went over and over everything I had decided to say and every possible question that might be asked, and Jim brought in students to help me practice. The night before the exam, we had a final rehearsal, and I was hopeless. I had lost all the continuity of the points I wanted to make. I had it all in my mind, but it was like an unedited film. At eleven o'clock, with A.J. in bed and Dottie almost asleep, I said, "Let's go over it one more time."

"Have mercy," Dottie said, but she poured herself more coffee, and we did it.

Finally, just before midnight, I got it right. The editing was done, and at one o'clock I fell into a deep sleep.

It is traditional for a doctoral candidate to offer refreshments to the examiners, and that was the first thing the committee and hangers-on wanted when they arrived. While Dottie gave them coffee and homemade cookies in the dining room, I was in a stew, waiting for them. Why did they need coffee on a warm day? Why did they take so long? Had they lost interest in me already?

At last, they all came into my room and sat down, and the professor who had a cold sat by the door where he could hear but would not be a danger to me.

I came up from a backswing and saw that all their eyes were on me. Jim Lackner nodded, and I began.

"A tree, like the one outside my window, is a common living organism. So common, we take it for granted. But its function of photosynthesis is really very complicated. When a circus seal balances a ball on his nose, very complex neurological and muscular processes are involved. But what plants and animals do is nothing compared to the incredible workings of the human brain, of which, to me, the highest example of function is language. As Chomsky has said, language is creative. There are infinite ways to express thoughts."

I went on to explain my experiments, which compared normal breathers with Dick and Muriel and Lily and me, all dependent on the life support of respirators. While I talked, Dottie showed slides on a screen at the end of the room. She had written out my main points on numbered five-by-seven cards that were propped against the reading screen which moves with the bed. I turned my head slightly on the pillow as a signal to change to the next slide.

Then Dottie collaborated with me in a dramatic demonstration to show that, as I approach normal breathing, I use more normal speech patterns. She stopped the bed, and I think some of the people there thought I was going to suffocate. But I frog breathed while I kept on talking, and then she started up the bed again with a rush of sudden movement, to show the difference in clauses and sentences between frog breathing and rocking.

"How many dissertation defenders," I asked the group, "can use themselves as proof?"

They seemed impressed. I felt wonderful. When I started to talk, I had felt like a wet hen, but once I was into my stride, I knew I had command of my material and of the audience.

After about an hour, I finished, and they all applauded. Then it was time for the questions, which I had gone over and over at Jim's house and again at home with Dottie. I braced myself for some tricky ones, but apparently I had explained the thesis clearly enough so that they kept to the general questions of why and how and what.

Jim Lackner's wife Anne, who had promised to ask me an easy question, came out with, "Were the subjects of the experiments right- or left-handed?"

I had never thought of this. After a moment of panic, I was able to say, "I don't know. They were paralyzed."

The three professors went out of the room to confer, while

I mentally bit my nails, and when they came back, they said to me, "Congratulations, Dr. Sternburg!"

Then Anne brought masses of flowers into the room, and Jim began to open bottles of champagne from the cooler in his car. They had been more confident than I was that I was going to make it.

Thank God, we had the wonderful brown van, and I had got myself used to going out in it. I wouldn't have missed the graduation ceremonies at Brandeis for anything.

Hank had just been appointed chairman of the board of trustees. He stood at the podium, tall and charming, and ended his opening comments by saying, "This is a personal privilege for me, because a very good friend of mine is here, Lou Sternburg, and I know the tremendous amount of work and effort that has gone into achieving his doctorate."

He smiled down at me, where I sat under an umbrella in the rain. My eyes filled with tears, because I was so proud that he was one of my best friends.

fifteen

I am lucky indeed to be surrounded by a number of close and treasured friends, who have contributed enormously to my survival and growth. Bobby read to me every day for six weeks when I was in the iron lung. Milt and Alan were among my first visitors at Mass. General. In a world gone crazy, they gave me a sense of constancy, which goes on, because of their regular visits. Alan has given me dozens of good sales contacts in the shoe business. Milt has been my confidant. I can tell Milt anything without his judging me, and over these thirty years he has supported me physically and mentally.

Al Clark, who was my neighbor when the children were small, can stabilize me when I'm shaky and anxious, because of his own strength and honest, calm devotion. We love each other like brothers. Henry Hacker has been my most constant and loyal visitor. He comes whistling down the hall, always ready with a new joke. Hank is an optimist who always looks at any situation as if the glass were half full, not half empty. He can put things in perspective for me, so that I can understand that I'm a normal person with normal emotions, who just happens to be rocking. As I age and reach a different plateau, he is honest and astute enough to show me that, although he is very successful, he too has gone through the same kind of trials, and that struggle is part of all our lives. When he talks about me at public functions, he boosts my morale by making me feel that what I have done so far is worthwhile.

Hank and Sonny let me use their staff to type my business letters. Dave, my dentist, my lawyers, Stan and Buddy, and my accountant, Jordy, all come to the house when I need them, and none of them has ever sent me a bill.

Women friends have shopped for me when Dottie is away and given me refreshing female company, which helps me to understand marriage and relationships between men and women. Elaine knows me better than I know myself. She comes to my aid in times of distress, and Dodo, Dottie's traveling buddy, can always give me a lift when I'm down, with her joyous outlook on life. Hank's wife, Lois, with her wide smile and her beautiful eyes under her cap of thick, dark hair, has opened the world of contemporary art to me and is always there when I need support.

All these people give generously, their time, their sensitivity, their knowledge, their encouragement, and they never ask anything back from me. Dottie is the most important person in my life, but without my friends I don't think I would have made it this far.

Dottie He still meets a lot of people and is always making new friends. They come to him from all over. He's a sort of magnet to them. They love to be with Louis because he makes them feel good, and he has the gift of knowing how to draw them out to talk about themselves, and then to listen. Our friends' kids drop in to talk about their triumphs and frustrations and to try out new ideas on him. Athletes who come here, prizing the health and strength of their bodies, learn from Lou how fragile health can be and how vulnerable they really are.

People bring him their problems. He's conquered this terrible disease, they think, so he must have some answers for them. And he does. Not always directly, but he shares his confidence and peace of mind, and he's witty and fun to be with. Although they may come in thinking, "This poor man, what can I bring to him that will help?" they leave knowing how much they have gained themselves.

He will continue to strive and try new things and exhaust himself and me, and get the most that he can out of his limited physical life and give the most that he can.

I shall continue to build my life around him, as I have done for the last thirty years. But I also want to try to expand my life, although I am limited by the difficulties of finding enough dependable help for Lou when I'm not here.

I would like to use my mind more than I do and be involved in something more challenging than my sales business here, but even a part-time job would be almost impossible. What if the help didn't show up or quit without warning, as they sometimes do? What if Lou got a cold, and I couldn't leave him?

I see other women doing exciting and important things, and I believe I could do them, too, and make a name for myself and be successful, but I have had to come to terms with the truth that this is not for me.

"You do more than anyone," people say. "Dottie, you're so marvelous."

But if Lou's illness hadn't happened to me, they wouldn't think I was marvelous. I'm the same person I always was, but because this happened, I've coped with it, as they would if they had to, and other people would tell them they were marvelous, too.

I would feel more marvelous if I had gone out into the world and made a name for myself at something I chose to do on my own. I didn't choose this. It chose me, and I accepted. That doesn't make me marvelous at all.

In 1981, the *Today* show did a television feature about me, which they called "Lou's View." They fixed a camera to the head of my bed, and a lot of the taped footage shows what my room, the walls, the furniture, the people standing by me, look like to me as I rock.

My environment moves back and forth in a regular rhythm, and my mind and spirit also move to a rhythm that makes me aware that I am part of the cosmos. Gravity is the force that keeps the universe together and stops it spinning out of control. Gravity keeps us on this planet and me on this bed. Gravity activates my diaphragm to seek its lowest level as the bed rocks, making my lungs exhale and inhale. Just as the rest of humanity plays its part in the orchestrated ebb and flow of the universe, so I, too, move to the eternal rhythm of my own private world. I am no different from anyone else, since we are all part of a mysterious and great celestial composition.

I have some setbacks still, of course. Sometimes when I'm alone at night, the pain and frustration are overwhelming. There are two voices in my head. One says, "Hold on." The other says, "I can't make it." Across the room, the clock ticks off the seconds too slowly, so when the night seems endless, I set little goals. If I can make it for one hour, I'll try for two, and then two hours becomes three, until at last a faint light creeps around the edges of the drawn shades, and I can make it for a couple more hours to the promise of morning and the chance that I may have a better day.

If I don't, I set myself check points. I'll hang on till breakfast, till lunch, till Dottie gets back from shopping, till David or Susie call. Survival isn't an extended process. It's the next minute and the one after that and after that.

There are still times when I am tempted to think about death as an escape, but I made my choice a long time ago, and I'm not going back on it. When you live with pain, it's either flight or fight. I could either flee from the pain through medication, which would have the side effects of jeopardizing my breathing and diminishing my perceptions of pleasure, or I can fight it by increasing awareness of pleasure to blot out awareness of pain.

One of the enemies is self-pity, and there is no instant recipe for getting rid of it. I just have to work at it, because I can't risk letting it get me in its clutches, although it's all right if once in a while someone says, "Poor Lou," to show in a comforting way that they know about my pain.

Depression is still a lurking enemy that pounces from time to time and settles on me like a creeping fungus. I can't bring myself to make any business calls. I don't want to read or listen to music—what's the point? I can't talk to my friends or family without complaining. I won't go out, and I don't want to see anyone.

Like pain, depression cannot be surmounted by a tremendous leap of will. It has to be tackled in tiny steps. I set myself short-term goals. I'm going to get on the phone and make two calls, that's all. Then I'll make three. I will play one game of chess. I'll listen to half an hour of music. I'll call Milt and ask him to stop by on his way home from work. I'll watch the news. If it's night time, I'll listen to a radio talk show for an hour.

When useless, negative thoughts start bombarding my head, I apply the meditation technique and let them go like air bubbles. I try to detach myself from "I want" and "I deserve" and deliberately think about someone else. Often it's my children. I love them very much, and I'm proud of the lives they are making for themselves. I want to see them settled, married perhaps, with children of their own. I want to see how things turn out.

I'm not afraid of dying now, only of a struggling, painful death, but I want to stick around for a while longer to see what happens. When I was a small boy, my father used to take me to see all the Red Sox games at Fenway Park in

Boston. I remember one game in which, after seven innings, the Sox still had zero on the score board. I wanted to go home, but my father said, "Wait, Louis. The game's not over yet. It's the final score that counts." The Red Sox went on to win that game, and perhaps that was the origin of my unfailing curiosity to see how things turn out.

I have to know: what now? After the Brandeis commencement and the party in my room for two hundred neighbors, friends, doctors, nurses, teachers, politicians—everybody, the unknown and the famous, who had helped me over the years to reach this day—it wasn't long before I was casting around for what I could strive for next. Soon, I am going to have the honor of working as a research assistant in the newly opened Ashton Graybiel Spacial Orientation Laboratory at Brandeis. Jim Lackner is working with NASA to solve such problems as why astronauts get space sick and how they can develop clues that will allow them to know, in the absence of gravity, exactly where they are all the time, upside down or right side up.

I also have been asked to teach frog breathing to respiratory paralyzed patients, and I hope to be involved in counseling with the handicapped.

When Al hears people complain about small things, he tells them, "You ought to meet a friend of mine, if you really want to see something to complain about."

He brought a man over last year who was very depressed because of imagined health worries and a few setbacks in his business. He wanted to throw up his hands and stop trying and get out of it all. Although we didn't talk for very long, he left here really shaken up.

"I didn't know the things that go on in the world," he told me, "what other people have to face. You've made me see how ridiculous it is for me to feel so sorry for myself."

A.J. was picked up by a priest when he was hitchhiking, and they got to talking about a priest's work and what he achieves.

"You've got to come and see this guy I work for," A.J. said, so the priest drove him here and then embarrassed the hell out of me by falling on his knees by the rocking bed and asking me to bless him. He said he felt very humble, but not as humble as I did to be considered a worthy channel for God's blessing.

Thinking about my life over the last thirty years has forced me to conclude that getting polio may not have been a complete disaster. Who would I have been if my life had continued on its pleasant track? What would I have done? I think that polio may have given me something to offer.

Trying to look at my life as honestly as possible for this book has tempered some of my idealism and forced me to face the whole reality. I always imagined that I would walk again—that was what kept me going. But I see now that I was looking through the same rose-colored glasses that made me pretend, when I was first in the prison of the iron lung and could still grasp the handholds, "It's like being in a jungle gym."

"Make a bluff, Louis." My mother's teaching was still with me. There is no doubt that maintaining the endless illusion that I would walk again was one of my strongest weapons for survival.

Now that I have finally dropped the fantasy and accepted the reality, I see that I may have found an even greater strength. To pretend that it's not always going to be like this, so I can stand it, is not as powerful as being able to say, "This is the way it's always going to be, but I can stand it." Other things have taken the place of fantasy—the search for knowledge and wisdom and the discovery of a deepening faith.

I don't believe that all of this just happened to me. I have faith that there is a purpose, because without the illness I might never have been aware of the closeness of a Supreme Being. I think it is some sort of grand design, in which my part is still unknown but will be revealed to me at the proper time. Meanwhile, one of my jobs seems to be to help other people where I can, mostly through their doing, not mine. I don't feel like an inspiration, but if they choose to find that in my situation, that's wonderful.

I still dream about standing and walking. Last night I dreamed that I was moving freely about in another room, in a different house. I could come and go. My body was young and strong, and I walked out of a door into a garden and woke with the feel of springing grass under my bare feet.